IMAGES
of America

Benedictine Sisters of St. Walburg Monastery

Several sisters fish on the Villa Madonna property in 1939. From left to right are Srs. Mary Anne Wolking, Regis Egger, Petra (Joyce) Quinlan, Perpetua Booth, Assunta Hessling, Frances Jacobs, Teresa Wolking, Judith Hock, and Bertilla (Mary Margaret) Bell.

On the Cover: Some members of the 1947 Holy Cross High School faculty are captured on the cover image. From left to right, they are Srs. Avila (Alice) McAvoy, Charlotte Rachford, Frances Jacobs, Julitta Ege, Mildred Obermeier, and Euphrasia Von Hoene. Sr. Judith Hock is on the back cover.

IMAGES
of America

Benedictine Sisters of St. Walburg Monastery

Sr. Deborah Harmeling
and Deborah Kohl Kremer
Introduction by Sr. Mary Catherine Wenstrup

ARCADIA
PUBLISHING

ISBN 978-0-7385-9062-2

Published by Arcadia Publishing
Charleston, South Carolina

Printed in the United States of America

Library of Congress Control Number: 2012949541

For all general information, please contact Arcadia Publishing:
Telephone 843-853-2070
Fax 843-853-0044
E-mail sales@arcadiapublishing.com
For customer service and orders:
Toll-Free 1-888-313-2665

Visit us on the Internet at www.arcadiapublishing.com

Dedicated to all the Benedictine Sisters of St. Walburg Monastery, present, past, and future, especially Srs. Evangelista Pfraengle, Irmina Saelinger, Catherine Bramlage, Teresa Wolking, and Betty Cahill, who organized and preserved our history

Contents

Acknowledgments

The history of the Benedictine Order of women and men goes back to 480 AD. Its rich history is foundational to those who follow the Rule of St. Benedict today. To the Benedictine Sisters of St. Walburg Monastery, recalling the names of their predecessors—Benedict, Scholastica, Walburg, Boniface, Hildegarde, Gertrude, Alexia, Walburga, Margaret, Lioba, Domitilla, and Hilda—is like remembering the names of their family members. This book carries on the Benedictine tradition of honoring and remembering those who have gone before us and those whose lives have formed this monastery.

One such person is St. Walburga, who died in the year 779. She was born in England into a family of the local aristocracy. At an early age, she was entrusted to the care of the Benedictine nuns in Wimbourne, where she eventually made monastic profession. Her relative, St. Boniface, was a missionary monk and bishop who set out to evangelize Germany. He asked for help from other Anglo-Saxon monasteries, and St. Walburga became part of a group of nuns from Wimbourne who answered the missionary call. Eventually, she became abbess of the monastery at Heidenheim, a double monastery of men and women founded by her brother, St. Wunnibald. The 10th-century legend of her life tells stories of her gentleness, humility, and charity, as well as her power to heal the sick through prayer.

This book would not be possible without the talents and skills of sisters in the more recent past, including Sr. Camilla Powers and the sisters who produced images and text for the 100th anniversary of this community. I am most grateful to our current photographers, Sr. Emmanuel Pieper and Sr. Mary Tewes, who not only take good photographs, but also organize them in binders so that I can find them.

Special thanks go to Deborah Kohl Kremer, whose expertise and experience gave me the nerve to undertake this task. And finally, thank you to the Benedictine Sisters of St. Walburg Monastery, who taught me to read and write and who said "yes" to this project.

Introduction

The story of St. Walburg Monastery of Benedictine Sisters began in the late 1800s. It is the fifth-oldest monastery of Benedictine women founded in the United States. Our spiritual roots reach back to St. Benedict, who founded monasteries in Italy and left us his teaching in The Holy Rule. For over 1,500 years, followers of this Rule make perpetual vows that bind them to the Roman Catholic Church and a particular monastery, where the members live in community, are faithful to liturgical and private prayer, and dedicate themselves to work. Each woman who enters a Benedictine monastery does so in order to seek God. Our search is done through prayer and community. We learn from the Rule to see Christ in those who are on the same journey with us.

The traditional motto for Benedictines is *Ora et Labora*, or "Prayer and Work." Throughout the centuries, Benedictines have worked and served within the enclosure of the monastery as well as outside the monastery. They founded schools, cared for the sick, offered spiritual guidance, and extended hospitality to guests. St. Benedict did not direct his monks to any specific work or apostolate of the church. Rather, he directed them to engage in manual labor and live by the labor of their hands. In his chapter on the tools of good works, he urges members to embrace the corporal and spiritual works of mercy. To this day, we are committed to his teaching.

The German Benedictine sisters who arrived in Covington on June 3, 1859, were members of St. Walburg Abbey, a 10th-century foundation in Eichstätt, Bavaria, Germany. They were courageous nuns with strong faith but little preparation for the life and work they embraced. Within the first 10 years of the community's presence in the Diocese of Covington, the sisters built their first monastery in 1862, founded St. Walburg Academy on Twelfth Street a year later, and sent sisters to Ferdinand, Indiana, to establish a monastery there in 1867. During the Civil War, sisters tended to soldiers camped near the monastery in Covington. In 1918, the sisters were recruited and "ordered" to serve flu victims in the Appalachian area of Kentucky.

Firmly established, the community continued to grow, opening Villa Madonna Academy and College (now Thomas More College) and moving the monastery to its present location in Villa Hills, Kentucky. From the very beginning, the sisters were educated and sent to teach and administer in elementary schools, secondary schools, and colleges in the dioceses of Covington, Pueblo, Cincinnati, and Lexington. Beginning in the 1940s, sisters were sent to serve in hospitals in Kentucky and Colorado. In the 1960s, sisters trained or retrained to meet new needs by engaging in pastoral and catechetical work, spiritual direction, social work, and counseling.

The pages of this book will give you a glimpse of the history of Benedictine life in St. Walburg Monastery and will show how the members of the community lived and continue to live out the vocational call "to seek God in the young and the old, the sick and the poor, the stranger and the guest." We are grateful to all who have walked this way of life with us and who have supported us on our ongoing journey.

The Benedictine sisters sponsor Villa Madonna Academy and Villa Madonna Montessori at our Villa Hills location. Other works at the monastery include counseling, spiritual direction, hospitality, art, and music.

—Sr. Mary Catherine Wenstrup, OSB
Prioress, St. Walburg Monastery

The Benedictine Sisters of Covington are descended from St. Walburg Abbey in Eichstätt, Bavaria. The 11th-century abbey, which is still home to Benedictine nuns today, is seen above. Many other American Benedictine women's communities trace their roots back to this monastery. It is named for St. Walburg, a Benedictine missionary nun who went from England to Germany to work with St. Boniface in the 8th century.

Mother Alexia Lechner (left), along with four other sisters from St. Benedict's Convent in Erie, Pennsylvania, arrived in Covington, Kentucky, in 1859. Their mission was to establish the presence of the Benedictine sisters and "take charge of the girls' school" at St. Joseph Parish. Mother Alexia then gave the 3¢ that they possessed to a poor man and had complete trust that God would provide for the sisters. Mother Alexia was prioress until 1889, when she was given the title Honorary Prioress for Life. She died on December 14, 1891.

One
Beginnings in Covington

In 1859, six years after the Diocese of Covington was established and a year before Abraham Lincoln was elected president, the Benedictine Sisters came to Covington. At the request of Bishop Aloysius Carrell, Mother Scholastica Burkhardt of St. Benedict Convent in Erie, Pennsylvania, sent the sisters "to take charge of the girls' school in the German immigrant parish of St. Joseph Church."

Between 1859 and 1906, the community grew fast. By 1862, the sisters acquired property on Twelfth Street in Covington and built a monastery. There were 12 sisters at that time. A year later, they established St. Walburg Academy for boarders and day students. In 1867, four sisters went to Ferdinand, Indiana, to establish a community and take charge of schools in that area. In 1870, nine sisters were sent to New Orleans. In 1873, five more sisters were sent to New Orleans to establish another community, and in 1881, four sisters were sent to Tuscumbia, Alabama, for the same purpose.

During that same time, sisters were asked to staff six other Catholic schools in the Diocese of Covington and one in the Archdiocese of Cincinnati. The first two prioresses of St. Walburg Monastery, Mothers Alexia Lechner and Walburga Saelinger, are seen in this chapter.

In the early 1860s, Mother Alexia was faced with a growing community. She made plans for the construction of a new convent even though the country was in the midst of the Civil War. Union soldiers were encamped near the Covington location and offered to help with brickwork for the new building. One of the soldiers got mortar in his eyes and was in danger of losing his sight, but the sisters prayed for a miracle and used a relic of St. Walburg to ask for her intercession. The man's eyes were healed. To show their gratitude, the soldiers made a financial donation so that a statue of the Blessed Mother could be purchased for the new chapel.

The photograph below, taken before 1909, shows the Benedictine buildings on Twelfth Street in Covington. From left to right are St. Walburg Academy, with its own steeple; St. Walburg Monastery, with a plain roof; the two-story St. Joseph School, and St. Joseph Church. The school building between the church and the monastery was torn down in 1930. Because it shared a wall with St. Walburg, it was necessary for the community to replace the wall at a cost of $2,000.

The chapel (right) was an essential part of the monastery. The sisters attended daily mass here and prayed the Little Office of the Blessed Virgin Mary in Latin. They also prayed the rosary in German. The monastery held yearly retreats for the sisters in this chapel. The first retreat in English was in 1893. The last mass celebrated here was on July 10, 1968, after which the sisters who had been living there moved to the monastery in Villa Hills.

Mother Alexia began construction on a monastery (below) in 1862 with $50 in hand. St. Walburg Academy, part of the monastery building, opened in 1863. It educated both boarders and day students. The new St. Walburg Academy building on the left was constructed in 1890. The all-girls academy operated until 1931 when the building became the home of Villa Madonna College, the diocesan college.

The 1879 *Catalogue of the Nuns and Convents of the Holy Order of St. Benedict in the U.S.* refers to Subiaco, a 40-acre tract of land "immediately contiguous to St. John Orphan Asylum" in what is now Fort Mitchell. It was a farm that provided supplies for the monastery in Covington. There were two houses there, "one for those who are employed in working the farm, the other for the use of the Ven. Sisters exclusively." The photograph above likely shows berrypickers at the farm. The sisters, with aprons over their work habits, are seen with farm workers and their families.

Mother Walburga Saelinger was the second prioress of St. Walburg Monastery from 1889 until her death in 1928. As Helen Saelinger, she was the first postulant received into the new community on March 16, 1860, at age 14.

Mother Alexia (front center) celebrated her silver anniversary in 1878. She is surrounded by sisters holding symbols of their patron saints. Mother Alexia holds a Roman Missal, her anniversary gift. Sr. Evangelista Pfraengle holds a quill, the symbol of St. John the Evangelist. Sr. Walburga Saelinger holds a vial of oil, representing St. Walburg, whose bones exude a healing oil. Sr. Benedicta Berns holds a cross, representing the cross and seal of the order of St. Benedict. Sr. Scholastica Wilberding holds a dove, the symbol of St. Scholastica. Sr. Gertrude Bauer holds a heart, the symbol of St. Gertrude the Great.

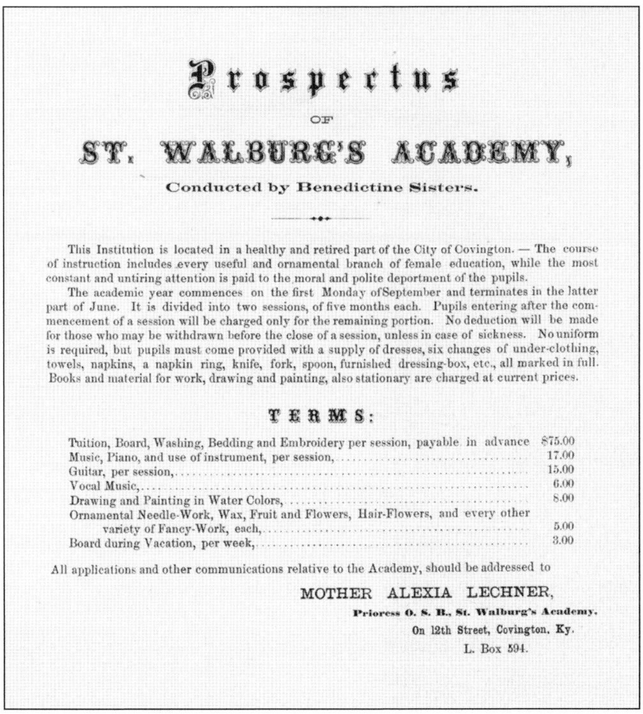

Prospectus

OF

ST. WALBURG'S ACADEMY,

Conducted by Benedictine Sisters.

This Institution is located in a healthy and retired part of the City of Covington. — The course of instruction includes every useful and ornamental branch of female education, while the most constant and untiring attention is paid to the moral and polite deportment of the pupils.

The academic year commences on the first Monday of September and terminates in the latter part of June. It is divided into two sessions, of five months each. Pupils entering after the commencement of a session will be charged only for the remaining portion. No deduction will be made for those who may be withdrawn before the close of a session, unless in case of sickness. No uniform is required, but pupils must come provided with a supply of dresses, six changes of under-clothing, towels, napkins, a napkin ring, knife, fork, spoon, furnished dressing-box, etc., all marked in full. Books and material for work, drawing and painting, also stationary are charged at current prices.

TERMS:

Tuition, Board, Washing, Bedding and Embroidery per session, payable in advance	$75.00
Music, Piano, and use of instrument, per session,	17.00
Guitar, per session,	15.00
Vocal Music,	6.00
Drawing and Painting in Water Colors,	8.00
Ornamental Needle-Work, Wax, Fruit and Flowers, Hair-Flowers, and every other variety of Fancy-Work, each,	5.00
Board during Vacation, per week,	3.00

All applications and other communications relative to the Academy, should be addressed to

MOTHER ALEXIA LECHNER,
Prioress O. S. B., St. Walburg's Academy.
On 12th Street, Covington, Ky.
L. Box 594.

This prospectus, most likely from the 1870s, clearly outlines the dates that school was in session, what the student was required to supply, the cost of tuition, room, and board, and the cost of additional classes in music or art.

This is the title page of a Grand Jubilee March, written especially for St. Walburg Academy in 1889, on the occasion of its 25th anniversary. It was composed by Salomon Mazurette, who was known as the king of Canadian pianists. His success was due to a spectacular performance style. His connection with St. Walburg Academy is unknown.

The 1911 graduating class at St. Walburg Academy (below) included Sr. Irmina Saelinger (back row, third from left). After graduation, she joined the monastery in 1913. Sr. Irmina went on to earn her PhD in education at Catholic University of America, and in 1928, she became the registrar and teacher at Villa Madonna College, where she served for 43 years. She was the niece of Mother Walburga Saelinger. Sr. Hilda Obermeier, who became the fifth prioress at St. Walburg Monastery, is to Sr. Irmina's left.

On July 18, 1916, the sisters gathered to celebrate the 50th anniversary of two members, Mother Walburga Saelinger and Sister Benedicta Berns. In addition to this golden jubilee celebration, two sisters were celebrating their silver jubilee, two more had pronounced their final vows, and four postulants had received their religious habit. After a mass at St. Joseph Church in Covington, the sisters invited all the guests to the convent for a banquet, and a program was presented in the convent yard by alumnae of St. Walburg Academy.

St. Walburg Academy's "Uniform One" was in a 1920s style and was worn by elementary students through the fifth grade. If the dress was less than 33 inches long, the price range was from $10.50 to $15, but if it was longer than 33 inches, the price range was from $14.50 to $22.50. The matching Red Windsor tie was 80¢.

St. Walburg Academy's "Uniform Two" was worn by girls in grades six through eight in the 1920s. Smaller sizes ranged in price from $13 to $17.60. If the student wore a Misses size, the price ranged from $18.50 to $27.50. Additional white lawn blouses of all sizes were available for $3.50 each.

St. Walburg Academy's "Uniform Three" was worn by high school students in the 1920s. The prices ranged from $15 to $23.50. In the spring and fall, a white middy was worn with the same skirt. Matching Windsor ties were 80¢ each, half- or three-cornered ties were $1.25, and whole squares were $2.25.

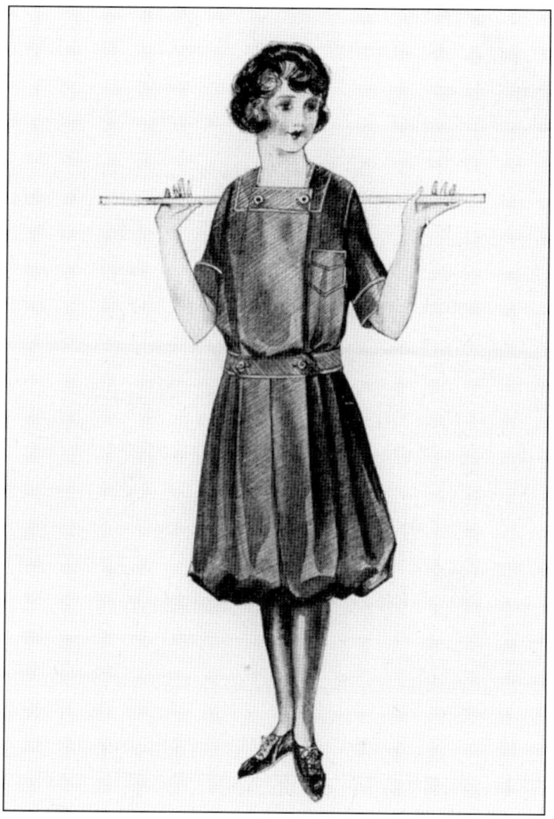

St. Walburg Academy's "Uniform Four" was the appropriate gym attire for junior and senior students in the 1920s. The mandatory uniform consisted of this black sateen jumper, which cost $7.50, and matching $2.25 sneakers.

The last graduating class of St. Walburg Academy poses in the garden next to the school during their freshman year. The sisters closed the Academy in 1931, after which the building was used to house Villa Madonna College, the new diocesan college for women. The class, a mixture of boarders and day students, appears to be wearing uniform three, the white middy.

The sisters of St. Walburg Monastery taught at St. Joseph School in Covington upon their arrival in 1859. The Benedictine sisters came to teach children of recent German immigrants at the parish school. The sisters taught girls in first through eighth grades and boys were taught by Marianist brothers.

This photograph from the 1900s shows, from left to right, Srs. Ida Platz, Ebba Krebs, Amelia Seefried, Sophie Saelinger, and Seraphine Welde, who were all early teachers at St. Joseph School in Covington and lived in the monastery next-door.

This photograph from the 1960s shows part of Covington's block of Scott Street to Greenup Street between Bush Street and Twelfth Street. At the time of this photograph, St. Joseph School was housed in the building next to the convent walled-in garden (in the foreground

of this image). Part of this city block is St. Joseph Church, with St. Walburg Convent and St. Walburg Academy next to the church. The original St. Joseph School once stood between the church and the convent.

In February 1968, after Villa Madonna College moved out of the old St. Walburg Academy building on Twelfth Street, the community decided to tear down the buildings, which had no market value, and sell the land to the bishop "to be used for the good of the Diocese." Due to the demographic population shift to the suburbs, the Benedictine fathers and the Diocese of Covington closed St. Joseph Church on July 5, 1970. The church, which was built in 1856 and was the third church built in the diocese, was then torn down.

Two

MOVING TO THE COUNTRY

The community's annals note that on "October 13th we bought on Bromley Heights a beautiful residence and 86 acres of land . . . We intend to build an academy there and later transfer the Motherhouse there also." The community called the new property Villa Madonna in honor of Mary under the title of Our Lady of Good Counsel. In March 1904, two sisters began living on the property and others began to visit. On April 14, former pupils of St. Walburg Academy met there and established an "Alumnae Association OSB" for St. Walburg Academy.

Villa Madonna Academy opened on September 7, 1904, with 10 boarders and day students. Ground was broken for the new academy on April 6, and the new academy building was blessed and opened on May 28, 1908. This chapter tells the story of Villa Madonna Academy and the Benedictine community's expansion on the Villa Madonna property. During that time, the next four prioresses were Mothers Margaret Hugenberg, Lioba Holz, Domitilla Thuener, and Hilda Obermeier.

The Collins family home, built in the late 1880s, sat on 86 acres high above the Ohio River. The house and surrounding acreage was purchased in 1903 and the sisters began transforming the house into classrooms, dorms, and a chapel.

This view from the Collins House looking west shows the bend in the Ohio River. Father Rhabanus Gutman, OSB, pastor of St. Joseph Church in Covington, found the Collins property and suggested the location to Mother Walburga. Upon seeing the grounds, she was easily convinced that it was the perfect location for a growing convent and academy.

The working farm behind the Collins House provided for the sisters and students, who first lived in the Collins House and later lived in the 1907 academy building.

In addition to finding the location, Father Rhabanus Gutman, seen here in front of the 1907 building, also suggested the name Villa Madonna, meaning the country seat of Our Lady. Father Gutman took a great interest in the growth of Villa Madonna Academy.

These sisters staffed Villa Madonna Academy in its early years. They include, from left to right, (first row) Srs. Blandina Farrenkopf, Benedicta Berns, and Cecilia Trainer; (second row) Srs. Scholastica Schnitgen, Anastasia Lechner, Monica Gabel, Vincentia Dolan, Romana Schwamm, and Magdalena Gerhard.

There were four classrooms in the Collins House, one of which is seen above. The classrooms and chapel were on the first floor. The second floor served as the student's living quarters; the sisters who taught at the school lived on the third floor. The academy opened in September 1904 with 18 boarders and seven day students. In Sr. Vincentia Dolan's handwritten daybook for the 1904–1905 school year, two of the day students were boys with the last name Lee, likely members of the Lee family whose farm was right up the road from the Collins House. The next school year, six of the day students were boys, but in the third year, there were no male students. Below is a photograph of 17 boarders in the 1904–1905 school year.

When Villa Madonna Academy opened in 1904 in the Collins House, Mother Walburga named Sr. Vincentia Dolan, seen here, as its first directress. She remained in this role until 1929. In her earlier years, Sr. Vincentia taught at St. Walburg Academy and assisted in the art studio, where she and Sr. Margaret Hugenburg taught the art of china painting.

The first Villa Madonna Academy building was completed in 1907. The building included classrooms, a chapel, and a cafeteria. The third floor was used as a dormitory for the boarding students. The bell tower atop the roof can be seen from many Northern Kentucky locations, as well as from across the river on the western side of Cincinnati. The building was the original site of Villa Madonna College, which was established in 1921 and remained there until 1929. The college then moved to Covington and on to Crestview Hills in 1968, when it was renamed Thomas More College.

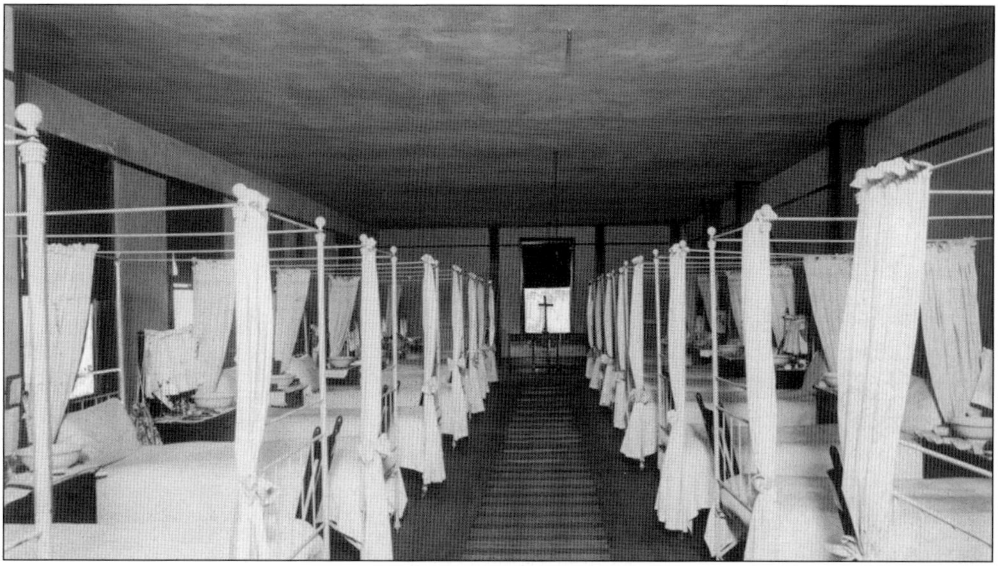

The third floor of the academy building was used as living quarters for the boarding students and the sisters who taught them. There were five rooms with curtained beds and washstands, like those seen here. Throughout the years, girls of all ages came from the United States, Central America, and other countries.

In 1911, Villa Madonna Academy held its first graduation. Seated in front of their younger peers are the four members of the first graduating class. One of the graduates was Katrine Adams (front, far right), who joined the Benedictine community and was named Sr. Miriam Annunciata. She went on to become Villa Madonna Academy's second directress, serving from 1929 to 1961.

A 1916 photograph shows how ice was cut from the ponds for use by the boarders and sisters at the academy. The ice was hauled by horse and wagon and stored in an icehouse on the property. The 1907 academy building is in the background.

Although the ponds on the property certainly added to its beauty, this pond was used for ice, boating, and ice-skating. However, the sisters suspected that mischievous dormitory students snuck out for an occasional midnight swim.

This 1920s photograph is unusual because the angle seems to show a fence across the lake. In other lake photographs from around that time, it is clear that the fence is actually on the ground close to one end of the lake. On the left is the old Collins House. On the far right is the Brown House, a prefabricated Sears-Roebuck classroom building (below) that got its name from the brown siding. It was donated by Eleanor Altenberg, a longtime librarian at Villa Madonna Academy until 1945 and a friend of St. Walburg Monastery and Mother Domitilla. The Brown House was used for additional classrooms from 1921 to 1958, when it was demolished after the new high school was built. Eleanor Altenberg lived on the St. Walburg Monastery property until her death in 1969.

In 1920, the Villa Madonna Club held the first of many fundraising festivals. Each year, a group of friends of the community organized it and the sisters cooked for it and worked at it. Usually held in July, the festival was discontinued in the summer of 1941. This 1920 photograph shows cars parked for the festival and was taken from the vantage point of the current monastery looking towards the 1907 building. The slope on the left leads to the Ohio River.

This statue of Mary and the child Jesus was donated to the community by Fr. Charles Persy, a diocesan priest from Pittsburgh, who was a relative of Sr. Vincentia. He taught at Villa Madonna College in the 1920s. The statue is on the hillside above the Ohio River. Hill slippage tilted the statue until 1937, when new stonework and a new lower pedestal replaced the worn, cracking pillar. Below, it is pictured as it is today.

Built in 1931, the Villa Gates (above), as they are called, welcome schoolchildren and visitors to the property. The gate and pillar were erected during Sr. Margaret Hugenberg's term as third prioress. Sr. Margaret (left), the first American-born prioress, was an artist and musician who, naturally, had an interest in beautifying the grounds. The gates were constructed by the W.A. Natorp Company.

In 1928, the Natorp Company designed the sisters' cemetery on the grounds. The St. Walburg Academy alumnae donated the crucifixion group in memory of Mother Walburga. The image below shows the original layout of the cemetery with the individual graves of the sisters. Prior to 1928, sisters were buried in Mother of God Cemetery in Covington. Mother Walburga was the first sister buried in this cemetery. A bronze plaque lists the names of all the sisters buried in Mother of God Cemetery.

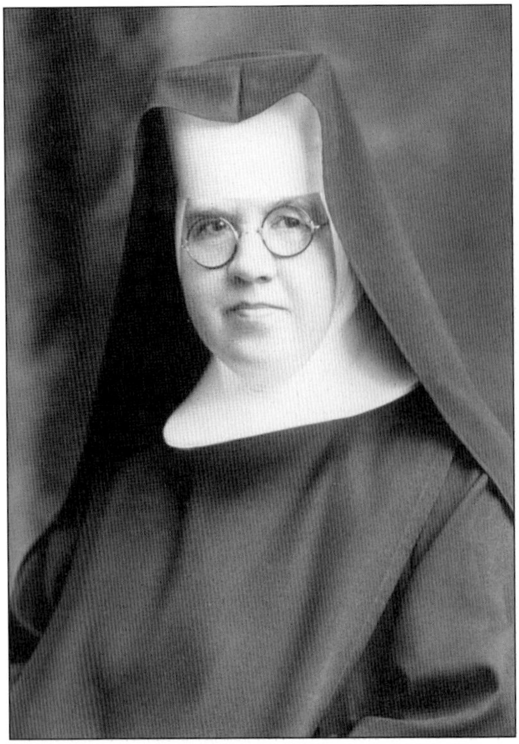

Mother Lioba Holz, born in Oberpfaltz, Bavaria, was the fourth prioress from 1931 to 1943. She oversaw the building of the new monastery in 1937. Because of the cost of the construction, Bishop Francis Howard decided that the chapel could be below ground level of the monastery "temporarily." It remained below the ground for 52 years, during which time children in Benedictine diocesan schools sold Christmas cards with the proceeds going to the chapel fund. It was not until 1989 that the funds were used for chapel renovation.

St. Walburg Monastery was completed in 1937. When it opened, it had 47 small bedrooms for sisters and two bedrooms for guests. The postulants and novices were assigned to 24 cubicles. Although the building was always intended to be the motherhouse for the convent, the whole community could never reside there at the same time. Sisters were assigned to schools and hospitals, which is where they lived most of the time. When the whole community did need to gather, they usually did so in the summer, so the nonresident sisters could lodge in the dormitories in the academy building. In 1961, the monastery's most populous year, there were 271 Benedictine sisters affiliated with St. Walburg Monastery. In 1968, an infirmary wing with 32 rooms was added to the south side of the building. The wing also included a large meeting room, which could hold the entire membership of the community.

After the monastery was completed on the Villa Madonna property, sisters who lived there and worked at other locations took the academy bus to their places of work or study. Seen here are Srs. Carlotta Ficks, Marcella Fedders, Evangelista Bankemper, Magdalen Rickling, Clementine Thesing, Lea McGuire, Regina Brueggeman, Louis Keller, Martha Feder, Callista Flanagan, and Louise Hillebrand. On the return trip, the bus brought the day students from the city to Villa Madonna Academy.

This early-1950s photograph shows, from top left to right, the Lee residence (now called St. Joseph House), the monastery, the priest's house, the Collins House, the academy building, the Brown House, and the tennis courts. The area in front of the academy building would soon be the site of the $1 million high school building.

Mother Hilda Obermeier was born in Bavaria in 1893, obtained her master's degree from the Catholic University of America in 1927, and taught in many Benedictine schools in the Diocese of Covington. In 1955, she became the sixth prioress. During this time, the "new building" was constructed. The story goes that Mother Hilda went to the First Federal Savings and Loan Association of Covington for a $1 million loan (below) and sat in an office until the request was granted. The sisters received permission from Rome to borrow money in order to build a new high school building. For the first time in the history of Kenton County, a mortgage loan was taken out in the amount of $1 million.

Villa $1 Million Mortgage Filed

1955

The largest mortgage ever filed in Kenton county was recorded Friday when a $1,000,000 mortgage was filed by the First Federal Savings and Loan Association of Covington in the office of William Bauereis, Kenton county clerk.

The mortgage was made by St. Walburg's Monastery of Benedictine Sisters of Covington in connection with the building program now under way at the Villa Madonna Academy, near Crescent Springs.

The mortgage was signed by Mother M. Hilda Obermeier, O. S. B., as president of the Benedictine Sisters.

Construction on the new academy building began in 1956. The above image shows the start of construction to the rear of the 1907 building. The image below shows the long-awaited new high school building, which opened in April 1958. In addition to the state-of-the-art science classrooms, the school had an art room with a kiln, a gymnasium, a large cafeteria, and even a bowling alley. This photograph shows the comparative sizes of the old and new buildings and the two-story hallway connecting both buildings. The 1958 building was made from yellow brick instead of red brick, which would have matched the 1907 building, because red brick was too expensive at the time.

Before 1960, the sisters raised sheep, cattle, and pigs on the monastery farm. Sr. Bernard Gripshover (above) was primarily in charge of the farm. The sisters also raised dairy cows for the monastery's milk and butter. Below, Sr. Bernard (left) and Sr. Kent (Betty) Cahill, a novice at the time, feed the cows inside the barn, which eventually would become the Villa Madonna Montessori School.

Sr. Laura Schollerer (left) and Sr. Agnes Ruschmann feed the chickens. In 1931, in the first years of the Great Depression, Sr. Laura started raising chickens, an enterprise she continued until the 1960s. A German immigrant, she was the first member of the monastery to live to 100.

The community discontinued farming on the property in 1967. In 1968, the barn and surrounding area was transformed into a summer camp for inner-city children. In 1972, the barn was renovated into classrooms for the Villa Madonna Early Learning Center, later called Villa Madonna Montessori.

The house built by the Collins family in the late 1880s was used as the school and home for the sisters before the 1907 Villa Madonna Academy building was constructed. At times, the house was also called St. Anne's. Later, the name was changed to the Senior House, because it served as the residence of the junior and senior boarding students for Villa Madonna Academy. After the boarding school was discontinued in 1979, it became a guest house for the monastery community.

Built around 1898, this three-story house was originally owned by the E.S. Lee family, and known as the Lee House. Later named St. Joseph House, it sits adjacent to the current monastery building overlooking the Ohio River. The sisters purchased the property in 1922 and the house was used as the residence for women in various stages of formation for the monastery. Since 1970, it has been used as a residence for sisters.

In 1938, the monastery acquired the Maegly property, which included this house, known as the Gate House. Originally, the caretaker of the boiler room and laundry lived there, and later, other employees lived there. Since the 1970s, the house has been occupied by sisters. The house is so named because it is adjacent to the gates marking the entrance to the monastery property on Amsterdam Road.

Over the years, this house has had several names, including the pump house, the men's house, the lake house, and Mannafold. It was built to protect the water pump adjacent to the lake in 1917. After 1930, when city water was piped to the grounds, it was converted to a dwelling for workmen. In 1969, it was used as a retreat house called Mannafold. This house was torn down in 1999 for the building of the new Villa Madonna Academy athletic center.

The oldest house on the property, known as St. Mary House, was purchased when the sisters bought 89 acres from the Brown family in 1928. This pre–Civil War house was occupied by a worker and his family for many years. In 1962, the community began to use it as a vacation and summer house for the sisters. It is located on the west end of the property and is now used as a residence for sisters.

The Knoll House was built in 1911 to replace an original workmen's residence that was destroyed by fire. It served as a home to workmen and farm personnel until 1968. Since that time, it has been used as a residence for sisters. It is adjacent to the Montessori school, which was originally the dairy barn.

Originally part of the Lee property, these two houses were built for the Lee sons and daughters around 1915. The sisters first called Cottage 8 (above) the Chaplain's House, as it was used for the priest assigned to the monastery. Most recently, it is used as an office for Sr. Aileen Bankemper's private counseling practice. Cottage 7 (below) was the residence of Eleanor Altenberg, the longtime Villa Madonna Academy librarian. After her death in 1969, it became a residence for sisters. These houses are located west of the monastery.

In 1984, SWM celebrated its 125th anniversary and the sketch above was created by local artist Thomas Martin to commemorate the milestone. It depicts the original monastery on Twelfth Street in Covington with the 1937 Villa Hills monastery in the background. Today, the sketch hangs in the Heritage Room of the monastery. The community celebrated by having then-prioress Sr. Justina Franxman (below, with her back to the photographer) and two former prioresses, Srs. Benedict Bunning (left) and Ruth Yost (right), driven in a horse-drawn carriage to the original site in Covington.

This 1970 photograph shows the front entrance of the monastery before the 1989 renovation. To enter the chapel from the front, it was necessary to go down the steps. By this time, the leaks in the front steps had caused the walls in the entranceway to deteriorate. The chapel, so central to Benedictine life, was not easily accessible by guests. The community hired John Pecsok of Indianapolis to design a model for the complete redesign of the community's worship space.

The new entrance to the monastery and chapel was made possible by removing the front steps and constructing a front entrance with a barrier-free walk to the ground-level chapel. The design of the front entry features a large stained-glass window created by Sr. Emmanuel Pieper and titled "Rivers of Peace."

These photographs show the interior of the monastery chapel before and after renovation. The original chapel was constructed to be temporary; 52 years later, oppressive summer heat, a frustrating sound system, and new liturgical guidelines for chapels led to an examination of the chapel space. The new chapel (below) was first used for Vespers on the first Sunday of Advent, December 2, 1989.

In 2000, Villa Madonna Academy completed its first new building since 1959, celebrating its new athletic center with this ribbon cutting. Seen here, from left to right, are Sr. Rita Brink, prioress; Sr. Victoria Eisenman, VMA executive director; Most Rev. Bishop William Muench, bishop of Covington; and VMA parents and students. The image below shows the three generations of buildings that make up the campus: the 1907 academy building, the 1958 high school building, and the 2000 athletic center.

Through the Center of Spirituality, which was begun in 2000, the Benedictine sisters offer two programs of spiritual reflection and development to the general public each year. Programs cover topics such as the communion of saints, the spirituality of Advent, the journey of Holy Week, the Eucharist, and other topics sharing the teachings of the Catholic Church and the Benedictine tradition. Seen here at a program on the Eucharist are, from left to right, Sr. Deborah Harmeling, Todd Barnett, Linda Young, Sr. Kimberly Porter, and Rev. Gerry Reinersman.

Monasteries of Benedictine sisters are flourishing throughout the world, especially in Africa. In 2001, Sr. Mary Catherine Wenstrup and Sr. Martha Walther traveled to Namibia to assist a young community. After their return, they organized a group of St. Walburg sisters to create a video on the spirituality and practice of the Liturgy of the Hours to be sent to Namibia. Those who worked on the video are, from left to right, (seated) Srs. Justina Franxman and Martha Walther; (standing) Sr. Cathy Bauer (working the camcorder), Srs. Christa Kreinbrink, Mary Catherine Wenstrup, Deborah Harmeling, and Kimberly Porter.

In 2007, two sisters from Namibia came to St. Walburg Monastery to study English, the psalms, budgeting, financial planning and management, and to experience Benedictine life in the United States. Srs. Justina Ndahafa Ita (left) and Mary Immaculate Iipinge are seen here celebrating their "graduation" from their studies before going back to Namibia.

In 2009, the Benedictine Sisters of St. Walburg Monastery celebrated their sesquicentennial anniversary after 150 years in the Diocese of Covington. As part of the celebration, the community partnered with Housing Opportunities of Northern Kentucky (HONK) to build a house on the east side of Covington close to the original monastery location. HONK provides opportunities for low-income families to own houses. The above image shows the October 3, 2008, ground-breaking ceremony for the House of Blessing, as the house on Trevor Street was named. Covington mayor Butch Callery speaks on the far right and prioress Sr. Mary Catherine Wenstrup is seated second from the right. The photograph below is from the July 11, 2009, dedication of the House of Blessing and shows the Beamon family with Sr. Mary Catherine (center) and two members of the HONK staff.

Three
Community Education Ministries

Through the years, the Benedictine Sisters of St. Walburg Monastery have taught in and, in some cases, established the following schools in northern and eastern Kentucky, as well as one in Colorado:

St. Joseph School, Covington (1859); St. Walburg Academy, Covington (1863, discontinued 1931); St. John's Orphanage, Fort Mitchell (1871); Annunciation Parish, Paris (1875); Holy Guardian Angels School, Sandfordtown (1880); St. Benedict School, Covington (1885); Holy Cross School, Milldale (Latonia) (1891); St. Henry School, Elsmere (1899); Villa Madonna Academy (1904); St. Anthony School, Forest Hills (1916); St. Joseph School, Crescent Springs (1918); Blessed Sacrament School, Fort Mitchell (1921); St. James School, Brooksville (1921); Villa Madonna College, founded by Covington Benedictines at Villa Madonna (1921); St. Paul School, Florence (1923); St. Therese School, Southgate (1927); Villa Madonna College moved to Twelfth Street in Covington (became diocesan) (1929); catechetical work began in Hazard (1947); Good Counsel Center and Kindergarten, Hazard (1948); Sts. Peter and Paul School, Danville (1948); Sts. Peter and Paul School, Twelve Mile (1948); All Saints School, Walton (1949); Our Lady of Guadalupe and St. Patrick Schools, La Junta, Colorado (1951); St. Ann Parish, Manchester (1953); St. Francis Xavier School, Falmouth (1954); St. Pius X School, Edgewood (Holy Guardian Angels Parish closed) (1954); Mary, Queen of Heaven School, Erlanger (1957).

The St. John Orphan Society and Bishop Augustus Maria Toebbe asked the Benedictine sisters to take over St. John's Orphanage in 1871. A facility was built that same year off Lexington Pike (now known as Dixie Highway) in Fort Mitchell, Kentucky. At left, Sr. Stella Kelz is seen with children on an outing to Coney Island in the 1930s. The undated photograph below shows about 100 students from the orphanage arranged from youngest to oldest. The Benedictine sisters left the orphanage in 1957.

In 1870, the Benedictine sisters were asked by the pastor of Holy Guardian Angels Parish in Sandfordtown to start a parish school. Sr. Catherine Bramlage, who worked there from 1917 until 1922, related that the sisters served in every capacity, including teaching, playing the organ, teaching piano, cleaning the school and church, maintaining the fire in the potbelly stoves, and even shoveling snow so the elderly pastor could get down the steps when it snowed. Above, Sr. Gertrude Menges (left) and Sr. Martina Kelly are seen with the children of the school in the early 1900s. Upon the creation of St. Pius X in Edgewood in 1954, Holy Guardian Angels closed. The photograph below shows Sr. Jean Regan with her class at St. Pius X in 1983. Sr. Jean taught there from 1970 to 1986.

With the increase in the number of German immigrants in the southern part of Covington, St. Benedict Parish was established on Sixteenth Street in 1885. The Benedictine sisters were there to teach at the school from its inception. Above, members of a 1930s graduating class from St. Benedict Commercial School, a two-year program attended by students who had finished the eighth grade, pose with an unidentified sister. The school prepared the students for work by teaching them business arts, including stenography, bookkeeping, and typing. Below, Sr. Josephine Voss, Sr. Bernardine Bergman, and an unidentified sister row a canoe through the floodwaters after the 1937 flood, showing how high the water had risen in the schoolyard at Sixteenth Street.

In 1891, Holy Cross School in Latonia was established. The Benedictine sisters arrived that same year, living in the lower level of the church and teaching grades one through eight. Above, Sr. Placida Gripshover (left) and Sr. Crescentia Kern are in the garden of the first sisters' house in the early 1900s with the school building in the background. Sr. Crescentia taught first grade from 1902 until 1952.

Holy Cross High School began in 1919, at the close of World War I, with a two-year commercial course. A year of high school was added in each of the next two years. Sr. Lioba Holtz was the teacher, and the first graduating class was in 1921, just two years after the school began. At right, Sr. Frances Jacobs works the school printing press. Sr. Frances taught at Holy Cross High School from 1942 until 1962.

In 1890, St. Henry Church was established in Elsmere. In the early years, the school was run by lay teachers, but in 1899, the Benedictine sisters were asked to take over the school. Four sisters traveled by train from Ludlow to the Erlanger depot to begin teaching. The first graduating class, in 1916, had four students. From left to right, Srs. Aurelia Rensing, Rosemary Howell, Pauline Warndorf, Regina Brueggeman, Bernardine Bergman, Loyola Busker, and Celeste Schreck surround a Ford Model T that was donated for their use.

Sr. Hilarine Deavy, the principal of the grade school from 1967 to 1983, supervises the end of the school day.

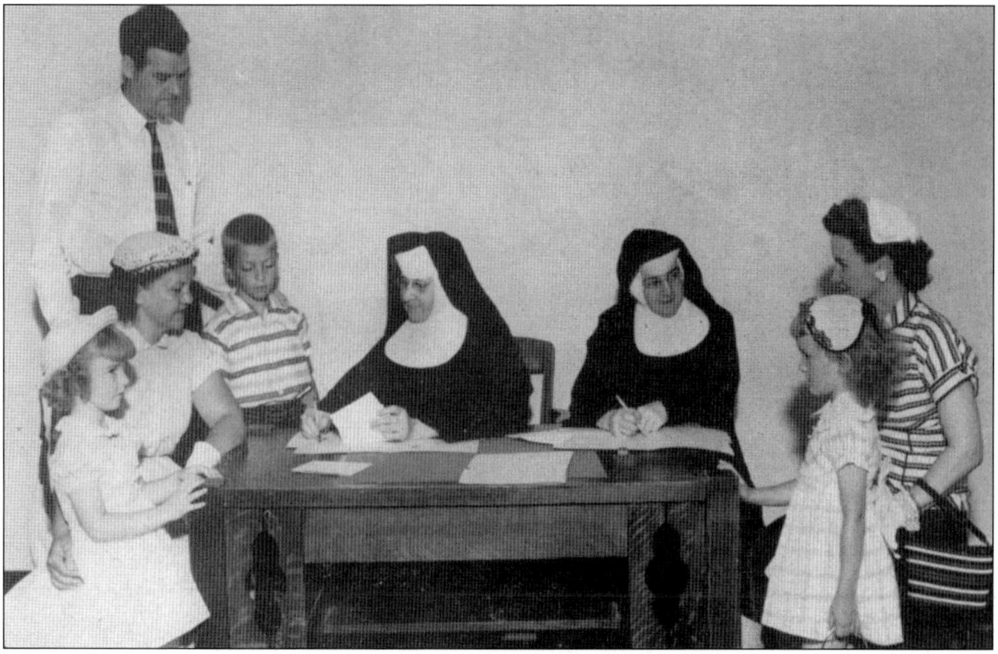

In 1933, St. Henry High School began with one grade, with a new grade added each successive year. In the beginning, equipment was scarce and it was difficult to keep the high school going. Sr. Pauline Warndorf was the first principal, serving from 1933 to 1942 and again in 1945. She remained on the faculty as a teacher until 1964. Above, Sr. Pauline Warndorf (left) and Sr. Damien (Pauline) Rice register children for school in the 1950s. Below, Sr. Clotilde Koenig, who taught in the grade school from 1914 to 1925 and in the high school from 1950 to 1956, conducts a history lesson.

In 1904, the community established Villa Madonna Academy as an all-girls school in what is now Villa Hills. In 1977, the elementary school became coeducational, followed by the high school in 1986. Above, Sr. Sharon Portwood takes advantage of the grounds for a natural science lesson with elementary school students. Below, Sr. Mary Rabe works with a high school student in the biology lab in the 1970s.

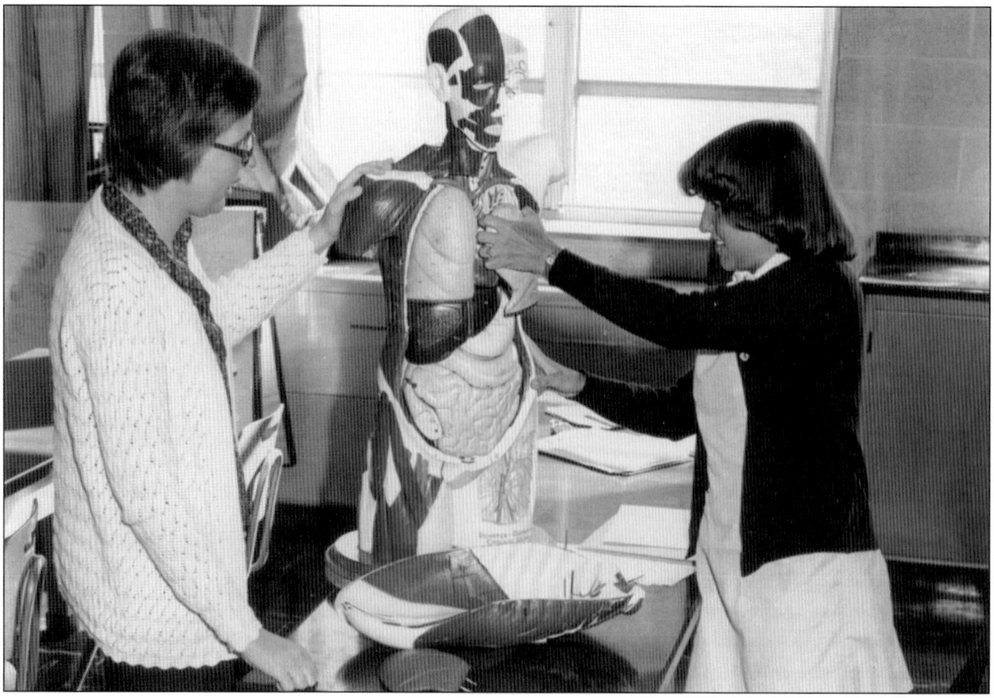

St. Joseph Church in Crescent Springs was dedicated in 1916. Two rooms in the rear of the church were used for classrooms. Fr. Herman Busse, the pastor, and Sr. Agnetis Green (right), who became principal in 1917, both lived on the monastery property and walked each day to the Crescent Springs school. The Krumpelman family drove them in their horse and buggy during inclement weather. Sr. Agnetis served as a principal and a teacher until 1932. In 1980, the Sisters of Notre Dame began to staff the school. Sr. Theodora Feldman is seen below with the class of 1937.

In 1878, St. Anthony Parish was established in Decoursey with the building of a small brick church. One room in the basement of the church served as the school. As the parish grew, the school was staffed by the Sisters of Notre Dame. In 1916, the Benedictine sisters staffed the school. When attendance grew, a room in the sisters' house became a classroom. Father Nurre relocated the parish to Forest Hills in 1928, building a two-room school and a new sisters' convent. In 1952, another new school was built and more Benedictine sisters came to teach. In the 1959 photograph above, Sr. Benedict Bunning poses with the seventh and eighth grades. Note the headphones used by some students. Sr. Benedict was a progressive and energetic teacher who was quick to adapt to new technology and new methods of instruction. The Benedictine sisters left St. Anthony School in 1988.

In 1920, the diocese created Blessed Sacrament Parish in Fort Mitchell. The church, two classrooms, and living quarters for sisters were ready in 1921. In the photograph above, longtime teachers, from left to right, Srs. Lea McGuire, Edward Sandheger, Mary Michael Voskuhl, Ann John Kotch, Hildegard Ricken, and Roseanne Hering celebrate the church's 50th anniversary. Sr. Edward was the last of the Benedictine sisters to teach at Blessed Sacrament School. For her retirement party in 1990, the faculty arranged an excursion to Riverfront Stadium and Sr. Edward, a noted Reds fan, was invited to throw out the first pitch. Below, from left to right, Fr. James Quill and Srs. Eloise Ring, Effie Whitten, and Edward Sandheger celebrate the church's 75th anniversary.

The congregation of St. James Parish was formed in 1866 in Brooksville, Kentucky. Mass was held in parishioners' homes until the church was built in 1914. In 1921, the Benedictines began staffing the school and were there until 1968. Sr. Agatha Fischer, who taught there from 1928 to 1957, is seen here at a first communion.

The sisters' house at St. James was used as a vacation house during the summers. Its rural location gave sisters a chance to relax in the country. In this 1950s photograph, some of the sisters enjoy the vacation time in Brooksville.

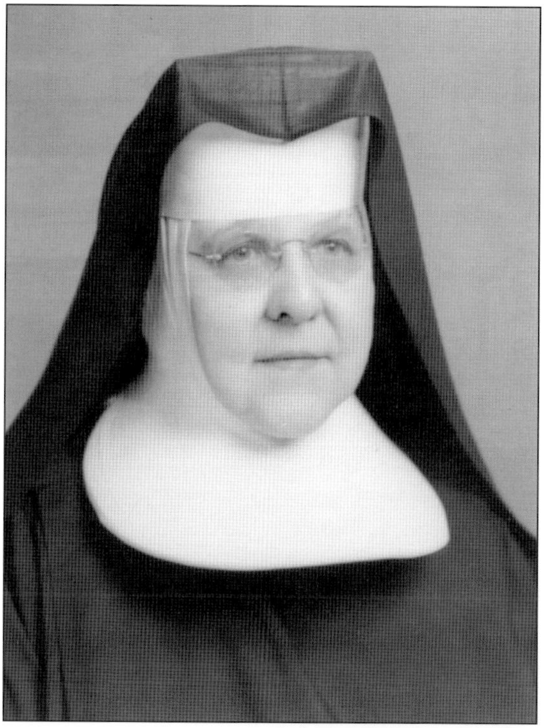

Sr. Domitilla Thuener saw the need for the teaching sisters of the community to have further education. In 1921, she was instrumental in the opening of Villa Madonna College in two classrooms inside Villa Madonna Academy. The sisters obtained a charter and articles of incorporation to operate the college and academy from the Commonwealth of Kentucky. Sr. Domitilla, who earned her doctorate degree in mathematics in 1932, was appointed dean. Faculty was recruited and seven students enrolled the first year. She remained with the college until she became the fifth prioress of the community in 1943.

This bus was used to transport students and faculty from the end of the streetcar line in Fort Mitchell to college and academy classes at Villa Madonna Academy. In this 1920s photograph, Ben Noll, the father of Sr. Thomas Noll, drives the REO bus that was donated by Sr. Evelyn Elsaesser's father.

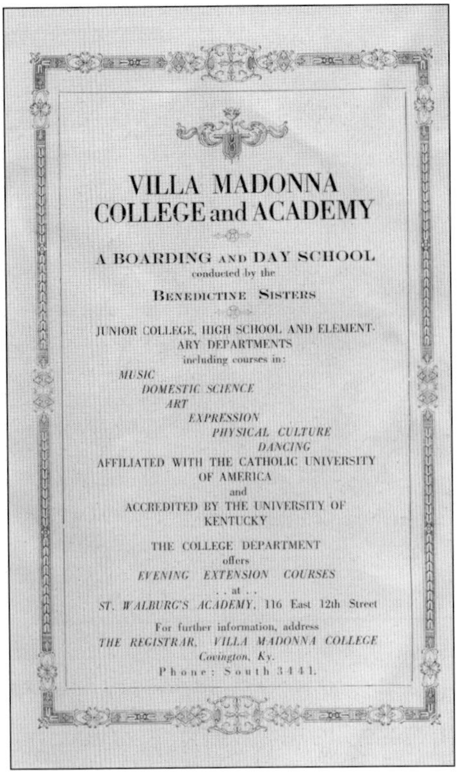

VILLA MADONNA
COLLEGE and ACADEMY

A BOARDING AND DAY SCHOOL
conducted by the
BENEDICTINE SISTERS

JUNIOR COLLEGE, HIGH SCHOOL AND ELEMENTARY DEPARTMENTS
including courses in:
MUSIC
DOMESTIC SCIENCE
ART
EXPRESSION
PHYSICAL CULTURE
DANCING

AFFILIATED WITH THE CATHOLIC UNIVERSITY OF AMERICA
and
ACCREDITED BY THE UNIVERSITY OF KENTUCKY

THE COLLEGE DEPARTMENT
offers
EVENING EXTENSION COURSES
. . at . .
ST. WALBURG'S ACADEMY, 116 East 12th Street

For further information, address
THE REGISTRAR, VILLA MADONNA COLLEGE
Covington, Ky.
Phone: South 3441.

This advertisement from the first Villa Madonna Academy yearbook, *Ros Maris*, dated 1924, is an example of how closely connected Villa Madonna College, Villa Madonna Academy, and St. Walburg Academy were. It illustrates the courses that were important for young women at the time—music, domestic science, art, expression, physical culture, and dancing.

By the late 1920s, it became evident that a centrally located college with a four-year curriculum including teacher training would best serve the diocese and the needs of the communities. The college was placed under the auspices of the bishop of Covington, and the three communities—the Benedictine Sisters, the Sisters of Notre Dame, and the Sisters of Divine Providence—were responsible for financing and staffing it. In this photograph, the college is located in the former St. Walburg Academy building on Twelfth Street in Covington. It remained in this location until it moved to a new Crestview Hills campus in 1968.

In 1851, there were three Catholic families in Florence, Kentucky, and mass was held in a parishioner's home. A frame church was built on Shelby Street in 1856 and it became St. Paul Church, with the first pastor appointed in 1874. The church had a school off and on over the years, but it officially opened in 1923 when the Benedictine sisters began to staff it. In 1925, the parish built a two-room school with a sisters' residence upstairs. Sr. Irene Schwartz (right) was the first principal and served until 1935.

Sr. Edward Sandheger, known for her love of the game, leads the schoolchildren in a game of baseball in the field surrounding the school.

Sr. Dorothy Kroetzsch is seen above in this 1962 first communion photograph at St. Therese Church in Southgate, Kentucky. The Benedictines began teaching at the school in 1927, the same year the parish was established. A new school and convent were built in 1952.

The Benedictine sisters served in various ministries in Hazard, Kentucky, from 1947 until 1981. They decided to establish a kindergarten at Mother of Good Counsel Parish in Hazard in 1947. The kindergarten was open until 1963. In this 1950s photograph, Srs. Wendeline Burkard (left) and Felicitas Weberding are seen with a student and his father in front of a town establishment.

At Sts. Peter and Paul, established in 1853 in Twelve Mile, students were taught by the Sisters of Divine Providence from 1916 to 1948, when the Benedictines arrived. Srs. Fidelia Hambaugh, Alberta Wolf, and Aloysia Kaufmann were the first sisters to serve. This photograph shows the church's unique rural hilltop location.

Although the Sts. Peter and Paul Parish in Danville, Kentucky, had been established in 1807, it was not until 1948 that the Benedictine sisters arrived to staff the new school building. Here, Sr. Louise Hillebrand (front), who taught art and music, is joined by (back row, from left to right) Srs. Julitta Ege, Rosemary Howell, and Genevieve Schulte in 1948.

In this 1958 photograph, Sr. Mary Peter Youtsey works with elementary school students at Sts. Peter and Paul School in Danville. The parish was in the Archdiocese of Louisville when the pastor, a Benedictine priest from Cullman, Alabama, requested teachers for a school he hoped to open in September 1948. He told Mother Domitilla that it "would be well for the community to become established in the Archdiocese of Louisville" and that the archbishop had approved his request. After visiting the parish and seeing the classrooms and sisters' house, Mother Domitilla said she would do her best to send three sisters, but that her promise was subject to the approval of both the community chapter and the bishop of Covington. Danville was said to be "a well known center of education containing Centre College." The Benedictine sisters staffed the school from 1948 to 1971.

Established in 1951, All Saints Parish in Walton, Kentucky, started out as a mission of St. Patrick's in Verona. The Benedictine sisters were the first teachers at the school. Seen here in 1951 are the pioneers of the school, Srs. Immaculata Campbell, Adelgunda Platz, and Paula Kurry.

Located in La Junta, Colorado, Our Lady of Guadalupe parish welcomed the Benedictine sisters in 1951. The sisters were working at nearby Santa Fe Hospital at the time and expanded their Colorado ministry to include education. This early 1950s photograph shows an All Saints Day celebration. Pictured in the background, Srs. Antonella Melchior, Aurelia Rensing, and Patrice Murphy taught at the school.

The Benedictine sisters staffed the parish school at St. Ann in Manchester, Kentucky, from 1953 to 1976. It was located about 45 miles from Mt. Mary Hospital in Hazard, Kentucky, where the sisters were already working in healthcare. Here, Srs. Aurelia Rensing and Irene Schwartz enjoy themselves on the school playground in 1956.

The Benedictine sisters conducted summer religious education classes for many years for the children of St. Francis Xavier Parish in Falmouth, Kentucky. In 1954, the parish elementary school opened with the Benedictine sisters as the staff. Here, Sr. Lea McGuire poses with first-graders.

The parish of Mary Queen of Heaven in Erlanger, Kentucky, was established in 1955. In 1957, a school, the first phase of the building project, was completed. The church was completed later that year. The Benedictines taught at the school from the beginning until 1977. The first sisters (above) were Srs. Dorothy Kroetzsch, Marita (Marilyn) Thiel, Alesandra Stuart, and Catherine Bramlage. Below, Sr. Catherine poses with the eighth-grade graduates in 1961.

In 1972, the former monastery dairy barn was transformed into classrooms to begin a preschool early learning center, which later became Villa Madonna Montessori School. At left, Sr. Mary Peter Youtsey instructs students in the 1970s. She became the school's director in 1977. Sr. Jean Scott, who joined Villa Madonna Montessori School in 1978, is seen below with younger children, ages three through six.

Four

Community Healthcare Ministries

In 1945, Bishop William T. Mulloy asked the community to undertake hospital work. Chapter meeting minutes from August 6, 1946, noted, "The most Reverend Bishop [William T. Mulloy] is anxious for us to take up hospital work because he wants us to expand and have an income over and above what the schools are paying."

This became an urgent request. The March 2, 1947, council minutes say, "Reverend Towell called late last night to inform Reverend Mother that the Most Reverend Bishop expects her to go to Hazard Tuesday . . . to sign the contract for the hospital." Other chapter minutes from 1946 show the community discussing another hospital, this one in Florence, Colorado, which would be established from a one-story building on the former Colonial Poultry Farm that was given to the sisters as a gift.

Community records are full of discussions about how to pay for the hospitals, how to renovate them, how to buy equipment, and how to train sisters as hospital administrators and nurses. The community eventually said yes to taking on two more hospitals—one in LaJunta, Colorado, and another in Irvine, Kentucky.

When the 1918 flu epidemic broke out, the sisters responded. The community record book says, "Today [Oct. 10] Rev. Regis Barratt [*sic*] of the US Army at Camp Zachary Taylor called at St. Walburg and demanded to have sisters sent to the Kentucky mountains to nurse the influenza sick. I [Mother Walburga] promised to send four sisters." On October 31, Sr. Alphonsa Spates (left) was one of the sisters who went to Lexington, Kentucky. On "November 1, Reverend Regis [Barrett] came back for four more sisters." Sr. Callista Flanagan (below), a postulant at the time, was also sent. By November 16, all of the sisters came back to the monastery. All were well except for Sr. Alphonsa, who had the flu. On November 16, schools were closed in Covington and sisters were called out to nurse until December 6, when the schools reopened. None of these sisters had training in healthcare.

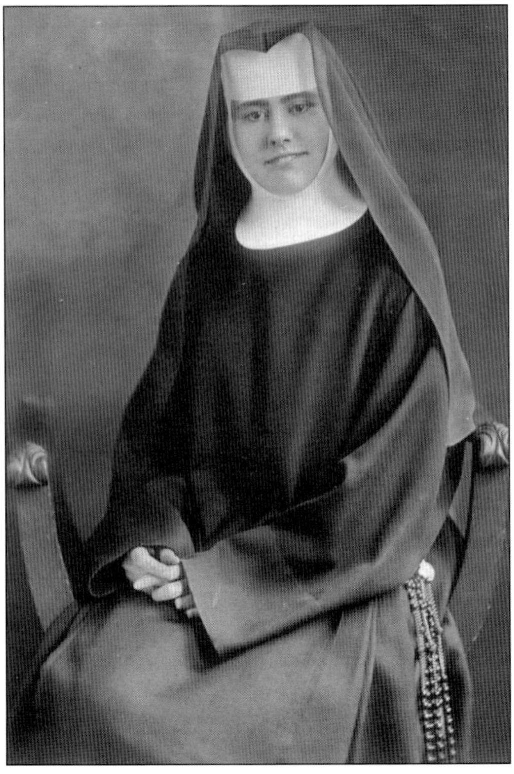

In 1946, the Benedictine sisters were asked to establish a hospital in Florence, Colorado. The former Colonial Poultry Farm (above) and surrounding grounds had been donated for this purpose. Sr. Stella Kelz and two other sisters were sent. The new 28-bed facility (below) was called St. Joseph Hospital and officially opened in February 1948.

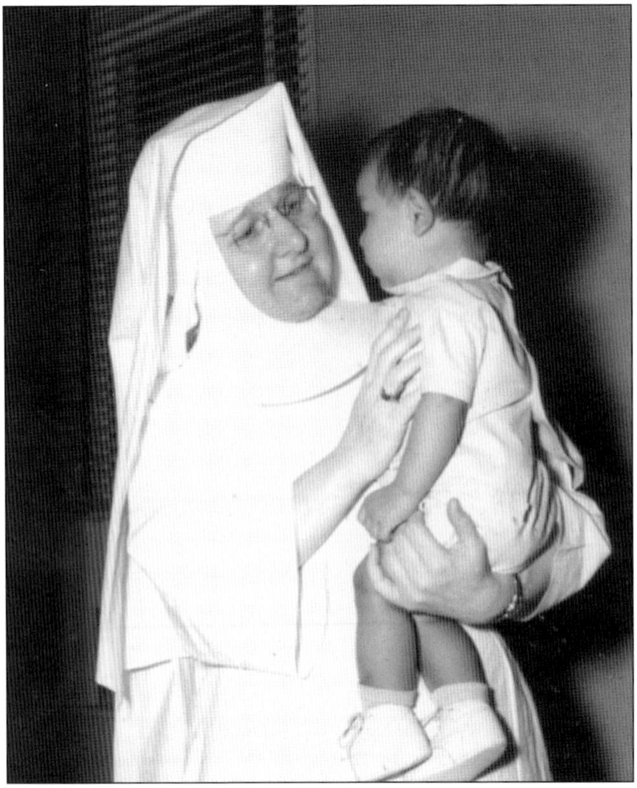

Sr. Stella Kelz, who turned a chicken hatchery building into St. Joseph Hospital, is seen here with a young patient. Upon her arrival in Colorado, she recorded in her journal that the building was empty except for a few chicken crates, and that outside she found a tin can and some rags. She began cleaning the woodwork with water from a nearby irrigation ditch. She was a nurse at the facility until the late 1970s. When she returned from Colorado in 1983, she served in pastoral services at Madonna Manor.

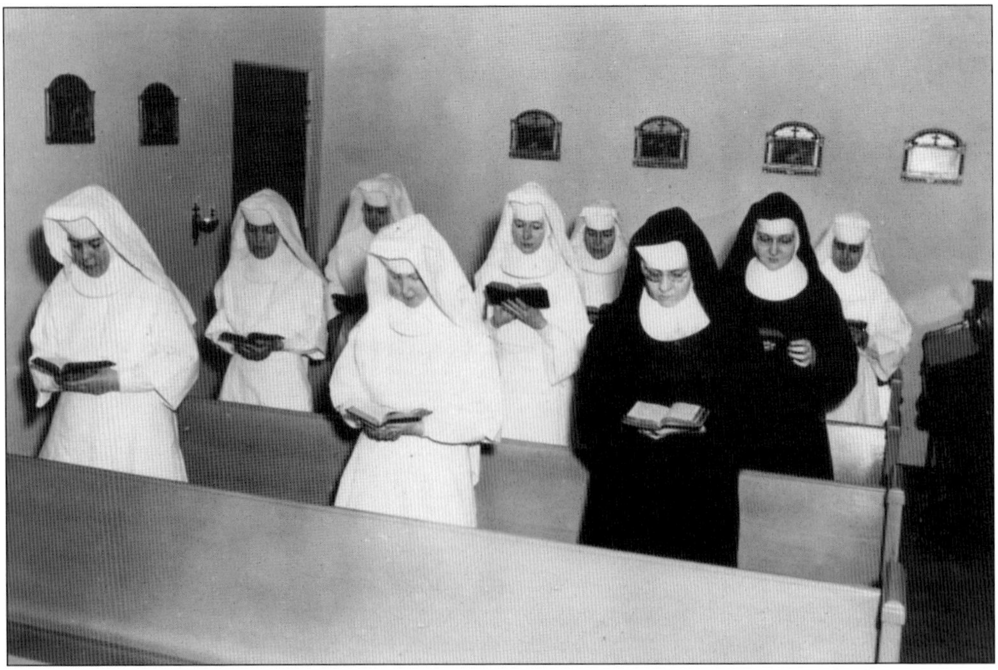

Many sisters from SWM helped staff St. Joseph Hospital, providing nursing and administrative services. Here, the sisters are shown in the hospital chapel at their daily prayers. Sisters in white habits were the medical staff, and sisters in black habits were administrators.

In 1947, Sr. Mary Gabriel Duffy and Sr. Barbara Dreier took over the operation of Mount Mary Hospital in Hazard, Kentucky. Sr. Benita Reis and Sr. Mary Gabriel are pictured here tending to an infant patient. Notice the lack of a standard hospital bed.

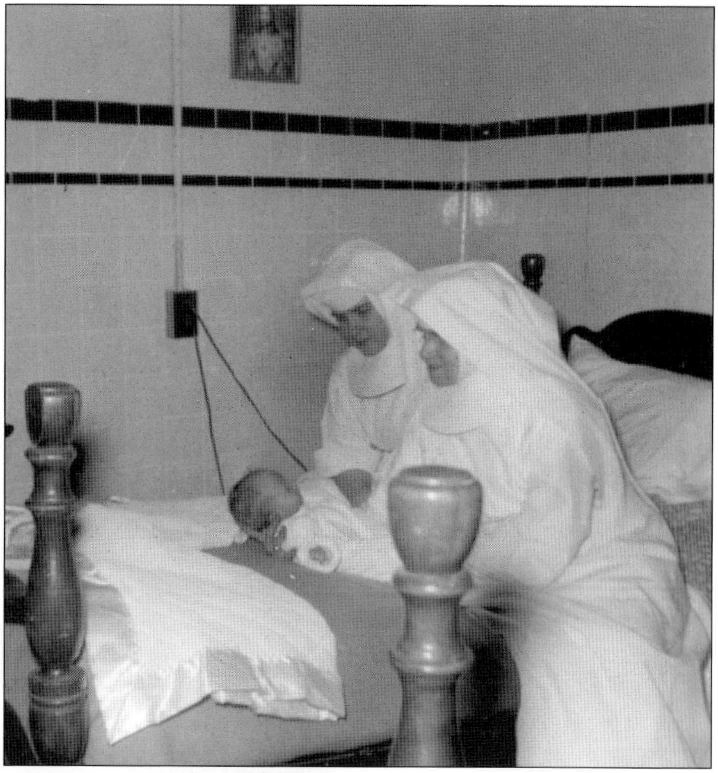

In this photograph, the Benedictine sisters and the church pastor are shown with Mary Breckenridge, who founded the Frontier Nursing Service as well as her own midwifery school. From left to right, they are (first row) Sr. Clare Bonfield, Mary Breckenridge, Sr. Mary Gabriel Duffy, and Sr. Thomas Noll; (second row) Sr. Wendeline Burkard, Father Anthony Kraff, and Sr. Felicitas Weberding. In 1967, the sisters turned over the 62-bed hospital to the Appalachian Regional Hospitals, Inc.

In 1950, the Benedictine sisters were invited to take over the Santa Fe Hospital in La Junta, Colorado. Until that time, the hospital had been for employees of the Santa Fe railroad only, so the sisters assumed a debt and began the renovation process to add an emergency room, an obstetric department, an operating room, and X-ray and laboratory facilities. At left, Sr. Callista Flanagan, who had wanted to be a nurse since the 1918 flu epidemic, directs the renovation process in November 1952. The finished facility is seen below. It closed on April 30, 1963.

On May 6, 1959, the Benedictine sisters signed a 99-year lease to operate Estill County Hospital in Irvine, Kentucky. Sr. Callista Flanagan was the first administrator. Some local residents of the city resisted the idea of a religious-based healthcare facility. Weeks after the sisters' arrival, a group of citizens filed suit to prevent them from running the hospital, arguing that the arrangement violated the separation of church and state. Over the next three years, the suit went all the way to the US Supreme Court, which ruled in the sisters' favor, making national news. Seen here at the dedication of the Estill County Hospital in 1963 after the ruling, are, from left to right, Srs. Xavier Anneken, Andrew Hellmann, Benedict Bunning, Ruth Yost, Esther Marie Hergott, and Annita Schirmer.

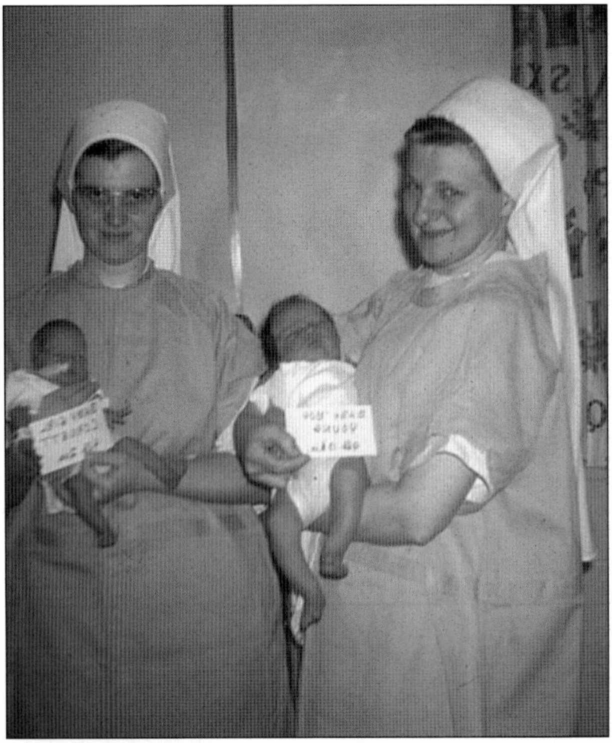

After the case was resolved, the Benedictine sisters became beloved members of the Irvine community. At left, Sr. Joan Gripshover and Sr. David Ruschmann tend to the newborns. Below, Sr. Bernardine Bergman, who taught classics at Villa Madonna College, visits with a pipe-smoking patient at Estill County Hospital. Both of these photographs are from the 1970s. In 1980, the hospital was renamed Marcum and Wallace Memorial Hospital to honor four local physicians, who happened to be two married couples. In 1986, at the request of the Benedictine community, the lease agreement was transferred to Mercy Health Systems, but Sr. Andrew Hellmann and Sr. David Ruschmann continued to work in Estill County and serve in parish activities until 2005.

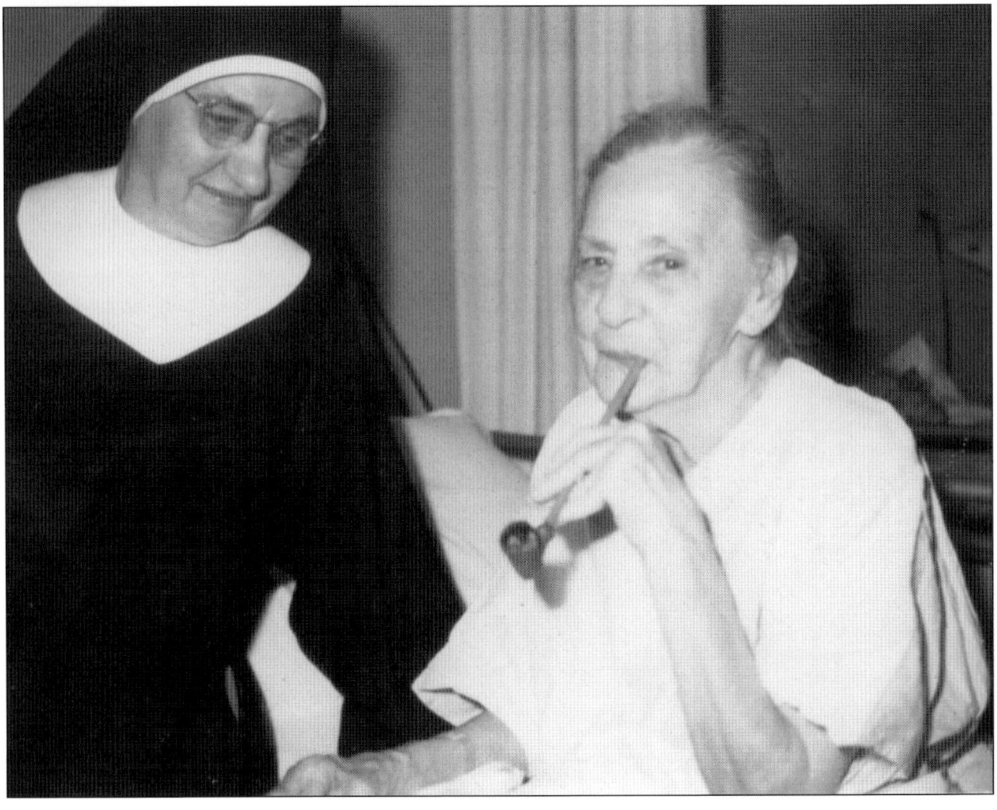

In 1961, Sr. Benedict Bunning (right) was elected seventh prioress of St. Walburg Monastery. At that time, a retired maintenance employee lived in the boiler house on the property. As the story goes, when he became too frail to live alone, Sr. Benedict took him to a nursing home in Cincinnati, but he did not like it and came back. This prompted her to think about the healthcare needs of the elderly, and the vision of Madonna Manor was born. Sr. Germaine Gehrig was the first administrator, followed by Sr. Martina Arnold. The 1970s photograph below shows Sr. Charles Wolking and Sr. Ruth Yost. The Madonna on the front of the building was carved by William J. Weberding.

Although many sisters were involved in the day-to-day operations of Madonna Manor, the sisters in this photograph lived on-site and are most identified with the facility. From left to right are (first row) Sr. Benedict Bunning, founder; Sr. Joseph Ruschmann, Madonna Manor's cook from 1964 to 1986; and Sr. Ruth Yost, who served in various capacities, including nursing, administration, and development work, from 1985 to 1998; (second row) Sr. Charles Wolking, the administrator from 1966 to 1999; and Sr. Geraldine Gajniak, who worked primarily as a night nurse from 1971 to 1995.

In the late 1990s, the community decided to transfer Madonna Manor to a corporation whose sole purpose was healthcare. In 2006, the community voted to sign a definitive agreement with Franciscan Health Services and the Franciscan Sisters of Sylvania, Ohio, to transfer Madonna Manor. This tile artwork hangs in the entrance of Madonna Manor. Created by Sr. Jane Mary Sorosiak, OSF, it features St. Benedict on the left and St. Francis on the right, with Mary and Jesus in the center. This artwork links Madonna Manor's Benedictine tradition with the new Franciscan ministry.

Five
Other Ministries

The Benedictine sisters served primarily in education and healthcare until the 1950s. At that point, sisters began to train for other ministries. In the 1960s, the Catholic Church issued urgent calls for missionary work in other countries and new pastoral needs emerged. After Vatican II, St. Walburg Monastery responded to those needs by encouraging sisters who had long worked in education and healthcare to train for new ministries. This chapter looks at the community's expanding pastoral, spiritual, and social ministries.

Sr. Margaret Hugenberg, born in 1878, began to teach drawing and painting in various mediums as early as 1900 at St. Walburg Academy. China painting was popular at this time, and Sr. Margaret had a large following of china-painting students. She was elected prioress in 1928. From 1931 to 1973, she taught oil, watercolor, and china painting to adult women. She is seen here in her studio around 1946.

Sr. Emmanuel Pieper taught art at Villa Madonna Academy for 41 years. With a master's degree in fine arts from the University of Notre Dame, she serves St. Walburg Monastery, the Diocese of Covington, and other organizations as a freelance artist. Her work, including oils, acrylics, watercolors, banners, and stained-glass window designs, graces St. Elizabeth Healthcare Hospice, St. Patrick and St. Barbara Parishes, and Thomas More College. She is seen here working on a mural for St. Henry District High School.

A diocesan supervisor of education in 1953, Sr. Wendeline Burkard (above) saw the need for the education of those with special needs. She began to press Fr. John Elsaesser, the superintendent of Catholic schools, about this. In 1955, she was directed to begin a special education program. She began in one classroom at St. Aloysius Parish for children of all ages. As it expanded, it became known as Our Lady of Good Counsel and was housed in the Mother of God school building. Around 1965, the school accepted students from Riverside School. When it moved to Fort Wright in 1970, the name became Riverside-Good Counsel. After retiring in 1973, Sr. Wendeline started Wendover, a group home for mentally challenged adults. She received many awards for her leadership and service.

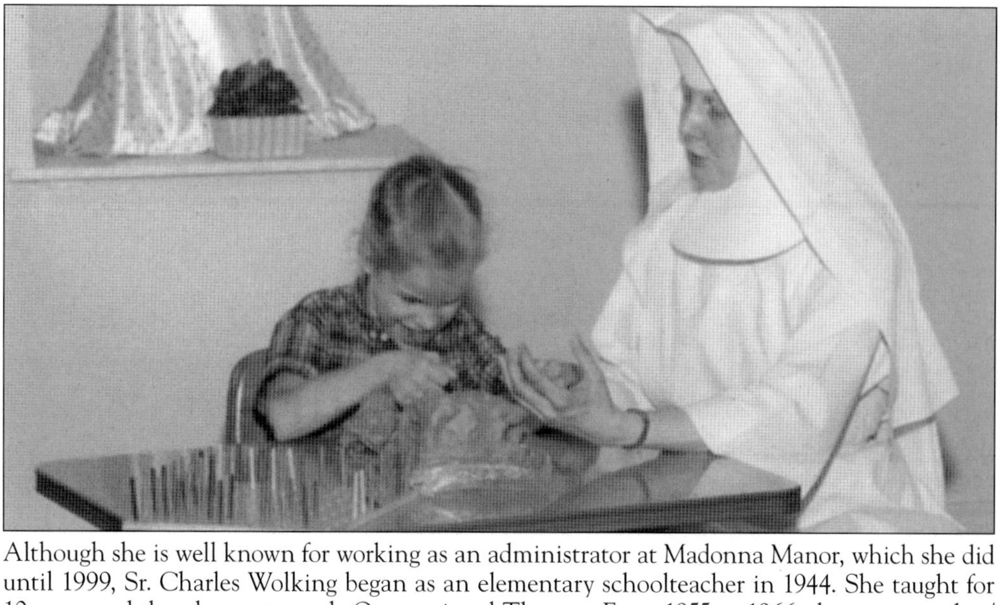

Although she is well known for working as an administrator at Madonna Manor, which she did until 1999, Sr. Charles Wolking began as an elementary schoolteacher in 1944. She taught for 10 years and then began to study Occupational Therapy. From 1955 to 1966, she was a teacher/ therapist at Redwood School, seen here, which was first located in two rooms at St. Benedict School. Srs. Ann Middendorf and Esther O'Hara also worked there.

In the 1960s, the Catholic Church expressed an urgent need for religious instruction and pastoral care in South America. Maryknoll bishop Edward Fedders, the brother of Sisters Mark, Viola, and Marcella Fedders, and the bishop-elect of Juli in Puno, Peru, came to Mother Benedict in 1963, asking for four sisters. Three sisters would teach religion in the public schools, where Catholicism was the official religion, and the fourth sister, a nurse, would establish a clinic and train native girls in nursing. Above, in August 1965, (from left to right) Srs. Annita Schirmer, Janine (Martha) Walther, Nicholas Jones, and Stephanie Manning left to train for their mission in Pomato, Peru. Sr. Annita (at left, second from right) was the nurse for this mission. In 1970, Sr. Andrea Vasquez was the last SWM sister in Peru.

The community discontinued farming in 1967, leaving a large barn and an area of land that could be used for other purposes. In 1968, the sisters began using the barn and the playground areas around it for a summer camp program for inner-city children, as "a way of sharing the land and its benefits with others." At left, camp counselors and children play on the tower slide. Srs. Henrietta Seiler (left) and Pauline Rice are standing and Sr. Anne Frisch is climbing the steps. Below, Sr. Henrietta Seiler reads with some children during a later summer program.

A teacher from 1952 to 1964, Sr. Margaret Mary Gough became assistant registrar at Villa Madonna College in 1964. She became the registrar in 1968 and served until 1976, when she became registrar at Edgecliff College. She holds a master's degree in education administration and a master's degree in theology. In 1981, she joined the Pastoral Planning and Research Office of the Diocese of Covington and was associate director for four years and director for 11 years. In 1997, she became associate director of development at Madonna Manor.

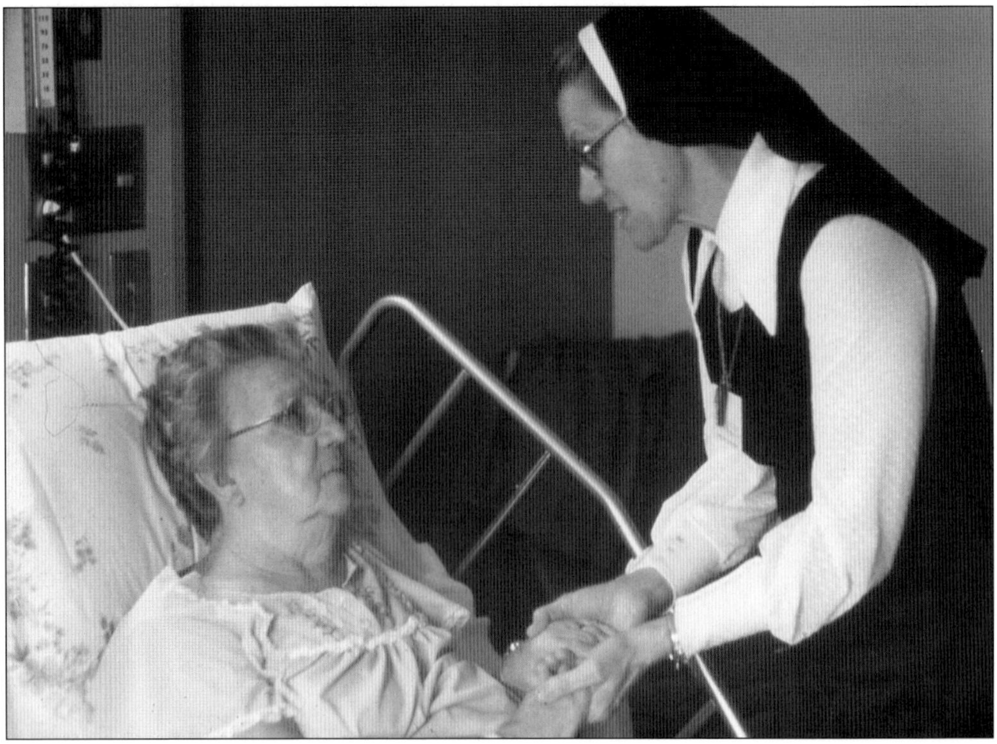

An elementary schoolteacher for almost 35 years, Sr. Valeria Schmidt began to work in pastoral care ministry at St. Elizabeth Medical Center in 1975 after completing a clinical pastoral education course. She updated her coursework in 1980 and spent 11 years in hospital pastoral care work. She was one of the first members of St. Walburg Monastery to engage in this ministry.

In 1976, Sr. Martha Feder left the field of education. She had spent 10 years as a teacher, six years forming new members in the Benedictine community, and 14 years as an elementary schoolteacher and principal at Villa Madonna Academy. She became associate director of the Worship Office of the Archdiocese of Cincinnati, where she served parishes as a resource person and helped produce liturgical publications as aids for parish leadership. Sr. Martha received a master's degree in theology and liturgy from St. John University, and her field experience is in liturgy.

From 1936 to 1972, Sr. Sylvester Shea taught in many schools in the Diocese of Covington. In 1977, Msgr. Thomas Finn and Catholic Social Services asked for volunteers to help adult Vietnamese immigrants who came to the area after the Vietnam War. Sr. Sylvester took courses to help her teach them to speak, write, and read in English. No Vietnamese celebration was complete without her, and, even after these friends relocated to other parts of the country, Sr. Sylvester maintained contact with them.

Because of the hospital work and religious education the sisters have provided in eastern Kentucky, they have always had affection and commitment to that area. Sr. Regis Egger worked primarily as a lab and X-ray tech in hospitals from 1949 to 1981. In 1982, she began to work at the Appalachian Servite Mission in Harlan, Kentucky. Her 11 years serving the people of Harlan County were perhaps the happiest years of her life. She was at home while interacting with coal miners and mountain people, sharing their poverty, hardships, and joys.

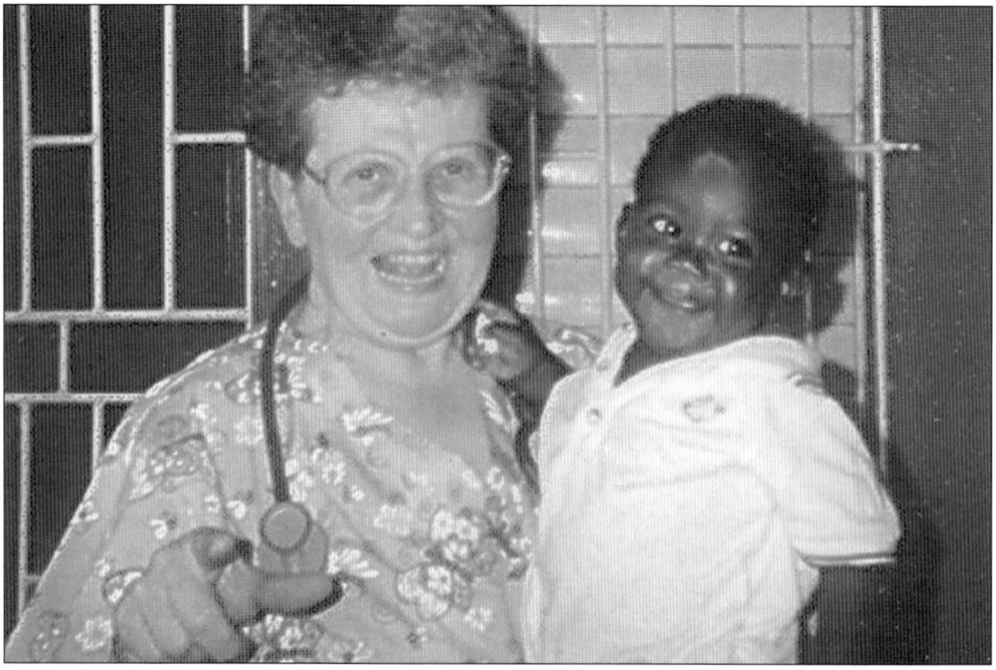

Sr. Joan Gripshover is another lover of eastern Kentucky. She received her RN from Good Samaritan Hospital in 1969. She worked in community healthcare ministries until 1982, when she studied to be a family nurse practitioner at the Frontier Nursing School of Midwifery and Family Nursing. Sr. Joan has spent almost 30 years in clinics in eastern Kentucky. This photograph was taken on a medical mission trip to Kingston, Jamaica.

Sr. Ann Middendorf spent 10 years teaching in elementary schools and 13 years as a special education teacher. In 1975, she became the first Benedictine to become a pastoral associate, working in two parishes, Holy Cross in Latonia and Blessed Sacrament in Fort Mitchell. In 1982, Blessed Sacrament Parish hired Sr. Ann to do pastoral outreach, which included the Rite of Christian Initiation of Adults (RCIA) program, and other duties requested by the pastor. She served there for 27 years.

Sr. Rose Rauen, who has her PhD in mathematics from St. Louis University, has served as treasurer of St. Walburg Monastery since 1982. From 1959 to 1981, she was an associate professor of mathematics at Villa Madonna/Thomas More College. She then became the codirector for a spiritual renewal program called RENEW for parishes in the Diocese of Covington from 1981 to 1984, the diocesan coordinator of ongoing renewal/evangelization from 1985 to 1987, and a pastoral associate at St. Agnes Parish from 1987 to 1991.

Sr. Mary Tewes became the first Benedictine sister to be appointed a pastoral life director. In 1987, the Most Rev. William Hughes, bishop of Covington, appointed her to Holy Trinity Church in Harlan, Kentucky. As pastoral director of the parish, Sr. Mary was responsible for day-to-day pastoral care and administration of the parish under the supervision of a canonical pastor (a priest).

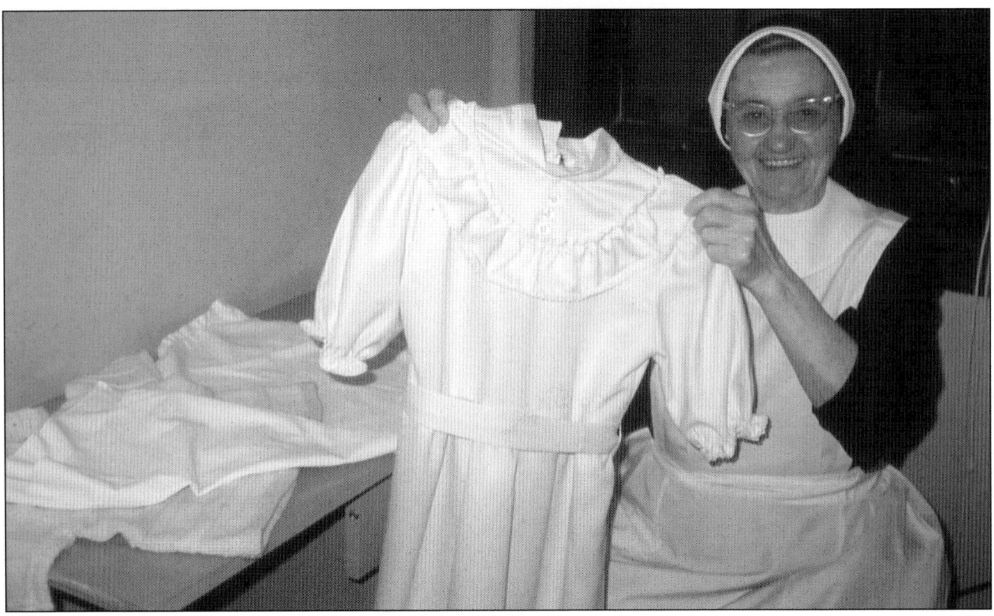

Sr. Benigna Gerstlacher was born in Germany in 1906 and entered St. Walburg Abbey in Eichstatt, Germany, on March 25, 1928. In July, she left for the United States to do missionary work. From 1930, she served as a cook, sacristan, and seamstress at many community missions. Although this was not what she expected when she left Germany, her service made it possible for others to do their work in schools and hospitals. With her missionary spirit, in her later years Sr. Benigna spent many hours making dresses and other clothing to support missionary work in other countries. She became a US citizen on November 21, 1963.

In 1991, Sr. David Ruschmann (above, left), a registered nurse anesthetist, and Sr. Andrew Hellmann, a lab technologist, joined Medical Group Missions, an interdenominational Christian mission. They volunteered to work in two-week medical, dental, and surgical clinics, helping people throughout the world with little or no access to medical care. Along with other medical colleagues, they worked in clinics in Ecuador, Mexico, Jamaica, Swaziland, and Peru. They are seen here at customs in Quito, Ecuador.

Sr. Dorothy Schuette (left) holds a master's degree in hospital administration, a master's degree in religion and religious education, and a certificate in spiritual direction. She has served for many years as a pastoral associate at Mother of God Parish in Covington. Active in social justice work, she also coordinates jail ministry for the Diocese of Covington's Catholic Charities. Sr. Dorothy is active in Catholic initiatives to abolish the death penalty.

Sr. Cathy Bauer came to the community with an associate degree in social work. She received her BA from Thomas More College and her master's in social work from Catholic University of America. She served at various social agencies in the greater Cincinnati area, including more than 16 years at Welcome House of Northern Kentucky. As the community vocation director, she continues to bring her love and concern for the poor, the homeless, and the unemployed. Her passion for social justice issues endures in her work with young adults. She strives to make the Gospel a message of hope and discernment for the common good.

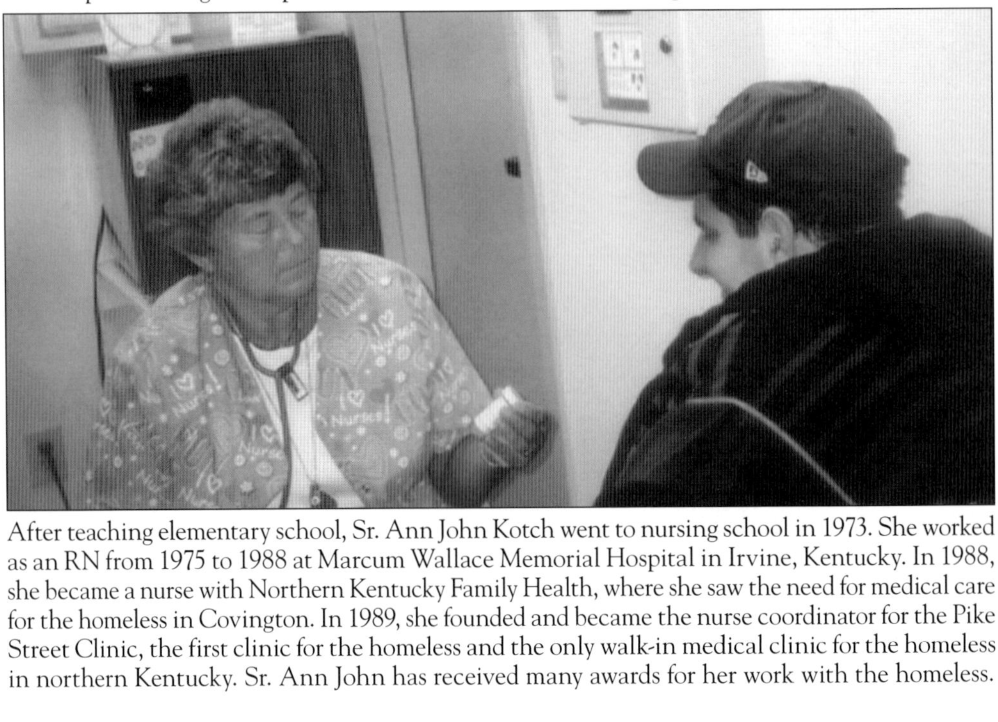

After teaching elementary school, Sr. Ann John Kotch went to nursing school in 1973. She worked as an RN from 1975 to 1988 at Marcum Wallace Memorial Hospital in Irvine, Kentucky. In 1988, she became a nurse with Northern Kentucky Family Health, where she saw the need for medical care for the homeless in Covington. In 1989, she founded and became the nurse coordinator for the Pike Street Clinic, the first clinic for the homeless and the only walk-in medical clinic for the homeless in northern Kentucky. Sr. Ann John has received many awards for her work with the homeless.

With an education and background in teaching, nursing, and psychology, Sr. Aileen Bankemper began working in 1983 as a counselor therapist at Catholic Social Services in Covington. She completed a PhD in clinical psychology from the Union Institute of Cincinnati in 1997. In 2000, she began a private practice as a clinical psychologist on the monastery grounds in Villa Hills.

Sr. Justina Franxman, who was prioress of St. Walburg Monastery from 1978 to 1986, studied at Shalom Center in Mount Angel, Oregon, to become a spiritual director. From 1987 to the present, Sr. Justina has accompanied many people on their spiritual journey. Two other members of St. Walburg Monastery serve also as spiritual directors.

Retired sisters engage in many forms of ministry. Elderly sisters meet frequently with students from the Montessori School and Villa Madonna Academy. Students visit in special seasons or on special occasions to entertain the sisters by dancing, singing, and showing off Halloween costumes. Seen here, from left to right, are Srs. Samuel Azzolina, Carmella Azzolina, Martina Arnold, and Andrea Collopy. Some Catholic schools in northern Kentucky have programs where children "adopt a sister" for a year, writing notes to her and praying for her. The sister may respond in writing or in prayer. At Villa Madonna Academy Elementary School's yearly Grandparent's Day, some sisters are asked to be a grandmother for children whose grandparents are not able to come.

Six

Faces of St. Walburg Monastery

The Benedictine Sisters of St. Walburg Monastery have touched many lives in their more than 150 years of religious life in the Diocese of Covington and beyond. This book cannot present photographs of all the sisters who have been members of the monastery, but it features many of the well-known sisters. Some are known for their stability and service in one place or one ministry and others are known for their multifaceted roles in many ministries. Some of the sisters are also blood sisters.

The four prioresses of the community since 1970 are, from left to right, Sr. Ruth Yost (1970–1978), Sr. Rita Brink (1998–2006), Sr. Justina Franxman (1978–1986), and Sr. Mary Catherine Wenstrup (1986–1998, 2006–present).

Sr. Irmina Saelinger, the niece of Mother Walburga Saelinger, received her PhD in education at Catholic University of America. In 1928, she became teacher and registrar at Villa Madonna College, serving there a total of 43 years until her retirement in 1971. From 1936 to 1953, she taught summer courses at Catholic University of America. She was the author of the book *Retrospect and Vista*, a history of the first 50 years of Villa Madonna/Thomas More College, and the *Capitol Spellers* spelling books that were used in Catholic elementary schools. On October 16, 1973, she was honored at Thomas More College, receiving the prestigious Thomas More Medallion.

Sr. Elizabeth Frisch earned her doctorate in mathematics from Catholic University of America. In 1981, she was invited to the Smithsonian Institute for a meeting of women who had received their doctorate in mathematics prior to World War II. She taught at Villa Madonna/Thomas More College from 1942 to 1974. When Villa Madonna College became coeducational after World War II and attracted students on the GI bill, Sr. Elizabeth's ability to teach practical mathematics was highly regarded.

Sr. Adelaide Feldbauer was sent to Holy Cross Church in Latonia as sacristan in the early 1920s, serving there until her retirement in 1987. She opened the doors in the morning and locked them at night, and, in between, trained hundreds of servers, prepared liturgies, sewed, cleaned, and performed numerous tasks in the church. In 1983, she was awarded the Benemerenti Medal by Pope John Paul II for service to the church. She died at the age of 101.

Seen from left to right, Srs. Amelia Wolking, Celine Flickinger, and Beatrice Flickinger were well known to the Villa Madonna Academy community. Sr. Amelia served as dorm mother from 1944 until 1979. She also supervised the cafeteria until the 1990s. Sr. Celine served nearly 40 years as cook at Villa Madonna Academy. Sr. Celine's blood sister, Sr. Beatrice, worked in the academy kitchen from 1927 to 1987, often alongside Sr. Celine. These three sisters touched the lives of hundreds of VMA boarders, students, and their families.

Sr. Miriam Adams, a member of the first graduating class of Villa Madonna Academy, was the second directress of VMA from 1929 until 1961. She was then administrator of St. Joseph Hospital in Florence, Colorado, from 1962 until 1970, and kept medical records there from 1970 to 1974. She later returned to St. Walburg Monastery, teaching special Latin classes and serving as a receptionist at Madonna Manor Nursing Home.

Sr. Rosalia Dixon spent 76 years in the community, many of them working in the laundry or waiting tables. She loved the outdoors and especially birds. When Sr. Rosalia could not be found where she was supposed to be, everyone knew she could be found outside, flitting around like the birds she resembled. No one knew the habits of bluebirds as well as Sr. Rosalia. She is seen here with a visiting owl from the Cincinnati Zoo.

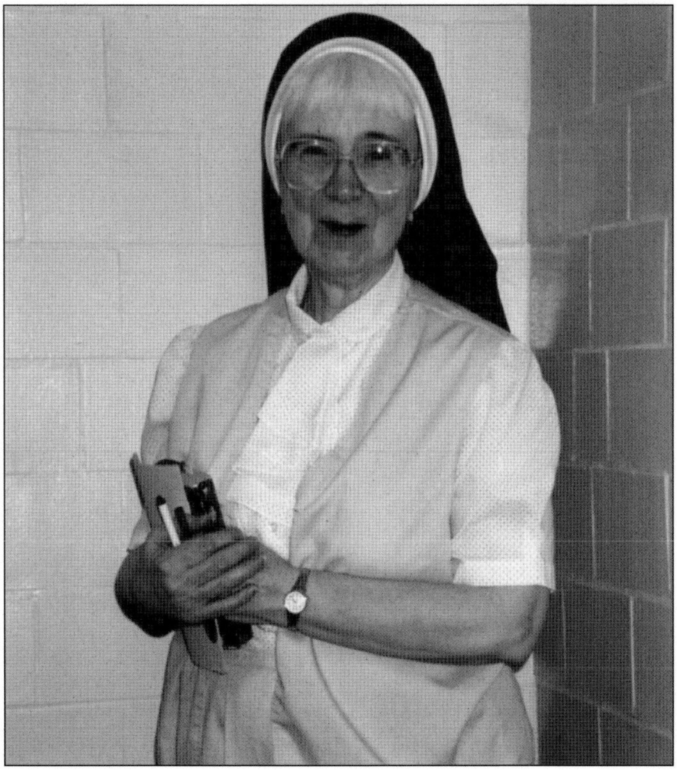

At times, it seems as if Sr. Andrea Collopy knows everyone in Northern Kentucky. Seen here at Villa Madonna Academy in the late 1970s, Sr. Andrea taught at VMA from 1950 to 1990. In 1986, she became sub-prioress of St. Walburg Monastery, and in 1990, she became the infirmary coordinator. She has many interests and even served as a volunteer EMT for the Crescent Springs Fire Department for 10 years. At any VMA function or monastery function, people always gravitate to Sr. Andrea.

Sr. Thomas Noll's father, Bernard, took care of the monastery farm, so she grew up in a house on the property in the 1920s. After Sr. Thomas joined the monastery, her contribution to the community came through her work on the grounds. In addition to a few years of teaching and hospital work, she also served the community in the laundry and by planting flowers and trees. At left, she is seen driving a tractor in the Villa Hills 1976 Bicentennial parade. She is seen below in the monastery courtyard.

The multitalented Sr. Marie Klingenberg taught at St. Henry High School and at Villa Madonna Academy before serving as principal and teacher at St. Henry. From 1973 to 1982, she served as treasurer of St. Walburg Monastery and performed other community tasks. She became the executive director at Villa Madonna Academy in 1982 and high school principal from 1983 to 1989. When she retired from Villa Madonna Academy, the Mothers' Club created the Sr. Joseph Marie Award, given to outstanding teachers, in her honor.

Seen on the right in this 1980 photograph, Sr. Nancy Kordenbrock is a Villa Madonna Academy alumna who has served at the academy since 1969. She started as a teacher and a dorm mother for boarders and became the Villa Madonna Academy high school principal from 1978 to 1983. She then spent three years teaching at Newport Central Catholic High School before returning to VMA as principal in 1986. Since 1995, she has taught full-time and part-time at the academy and worked with the alumni association in many capacities.

Sr. Grace Zimmer served as a musician and a teacher in many schools. She and Sr. Irene Schwartz were pioneers at St. Paul School in Florence, Kentucky, in 1923. She spent 30 years at St. Therese School in Southgate as a musician before becoming a music and religion teacher at Villa Madonna Academy from 1959 until 1978. After retiring, she enjoyed being the organist at Madonna Manor.

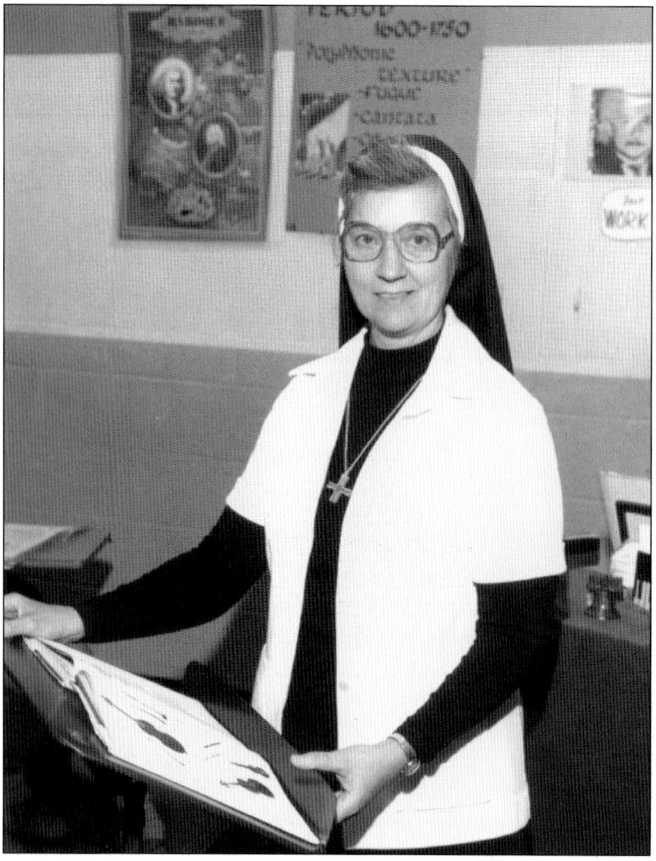

From 1953 to 1967 and 1971 to 1983, Sr. Mary Carol Hellmann, who has a master of music degree from the Catholic University of America, played the organ and taught at many parishes in northern Kentucky. She taught at Villa Madonna Academy from 1967 to 1974 and from 1983 to 2003. She was also the adult choir director at St. Paul Parish in Florence, Kentucky, from 1981 to 1991, and the adult choir director and organist at St. Benedict Parish in Covington until 1996. She currently gives private piano lessons, volunteers as the archivist at Villa Madonna Academy, coordinates hospitality at the monastery guesthouse, and is one of the organists at the monastery.

From 1943 to 1996, Sr. Teresa Wolking, who has a master of arts degree in English and comparative philology from Catholic University of America, taught at St. Henry High School, Holy Cross High School, and Villa Madonna Academy. In addition to teaching, she served as assistant principal at VMA and as principal at St. Henry and Holy Cross High Schools. She was the community archivist from 1971 to 2006, beginning the process of organizing and preserving the community's history and heritage. Her students remember her fondly for her lively teaching style, her passion for literature and her wide reading interests. Sr. Teresa is seen here in the community archives.

At the time of this writing, Srs. Carmella and Samuel Azzolina are both over 100 years old and spent a combined 88 years teaching at Holy Cross High School. They are pictured here with the Most Rev. Roger Foys, Bishop of Covington. Sr. Carmella (far right) was born in 1909, and Sr. Samuel (middle) was born in 1912. Their mother died when they were very young, and their father brought them to board at Villa Madonna Academy. Sr. Carmella entered St. Walburg Monastery in 1934, Sr. Samuel in 1940. Sr. Carmella taught at VMA for 22 years, and Sr. Samuel taught at St. Benedict Commercial High School, St. Henry High School, and VMA.

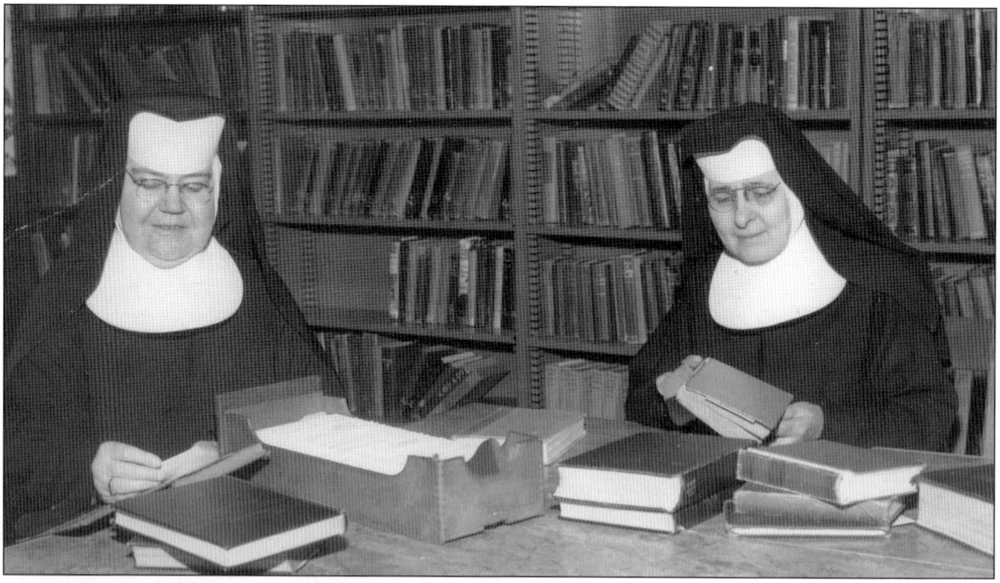

Sr. Mildred Obermeier (above, right) and Sr. Blanche Raker are seen here in the St. Henry High School library in the 1950s. Sr. Blanche was known as a rigorous English teacher. In her retirement, she wrote letters to shut-ins and prisoners. Sr. Mildred spent 28 years as the librarian at Holy Cross High School and 12 years as the librarian at St. Henry High School. After her retirement in 1979, she tutored students in Latin and German at Villa Madonna Academy until her death in 1983.

Sr. Esther O'Hara (left) taught in many elementary schools in northern Kentucky and served as the librarian at Bishop Howard School and at St. Lawrence School in Price Hill, Ohio. For four years, she was the transportation director at the monastery. In 1988, she became a freelance storyteller, ventriloquist, and balloon sculptor. Sr. Esther has performed at numerous schools—including in this photograph, at St. Joseph School in Crescent Springs—and events, including the Appalachian Festival, where she received an award for storytelling. Sr. Esther was also an enthusiastic volunteer at the Cincinnati Zoo.

Srs. Marcella, Mark, and Viola Fedders were three sisters from a Covington family of 13 siblings. Two of their brothers became Maryknoll Missionaries. Sr. Marcella (left) was a talented musician and created musical compositions. She taught at Villa Madonna College for 38 years. Sr. Mark (center) taught elementary school from 1929 to 1971 and Sr. Viola (right) was an elementary schoolteacher from 1925 to 1967.

Srs. Veronica (left) and Anselma Weibel were half-sisters, both born in Leipferdingen, Baden, Germany. They immigrated to the United States in the early 1920s and joined the monastery. Sr. Veronica was known for her cooking and baking and she served at Villa Madonna College in Covington for 29 years. There are many stories about her generosity toward transient men who knocked on the door looking for food. In 1968, Sr. Veronica came to the monastery and assisted in baking and cooking there. Sr. Anselma served the community in various capacities as sacristan, keeping house and caring for children.

Sr. Raymond Fessler (left) was the oldest of four children. She worked in business for some time before entering St. Walburg Monastery and worked as a bookkeeper in the community's hospitals from 1947 to 1972. When the hospitals closed, she returned to the monastery and assisted with housekeeping and other services, acting as the assistant sacristan with specialty in flowers. Sr. Monica Fessler came to the community two years after Sr. Raymond, spending some time as a bookkeeper in two community hospitals and working as sacristan at St. Walburg Monastery.

Srs. Louis (left) and Adele Keller were born in Lexington, Kentucky. They had three other siblings. Sr. Louis, the youngest, was named in honor of her brother, Father Louis Keller. Sr. Adele was the third of five children and outlived all of her siblings. She taught the middle grades at St. Benedict, St. Joseph, Crescent Springs, Blessed Sacrament, and for 26 years at St. Henry. When her niece needed a kidney, Sr. Adele offered to be a donor. Sr. Louis was the librarian at Villa Madonna Academy from 1945 to 1990. From 1952 to 1972, she was also the monastery librarian.

There were nine children in the Anneken family and four of them became members of St. Walburg Monastery. Sr. Gemma (left), the first to enter the community, was known as an excellent teacher and taught in many schools in the Covington diocese. Sr. Clarita (second from left) entered next and taught at St. Henry, Holy Cross, and VMA high schools for 63 years. Sr. Xavier (second from right) was the last to enter the community. She served as accountant and office manager at Mt. Mary Hospital; accountant and business manager at Estill County Hospital in Kentucky, and accountant at St. Walburg Monastery in Colorado. She also worked in the business office at St. Joseph Hospital. From 1983 to 2011, she was the transportation assistant and then the transportation director at the monastery. Sr. Juanita (right) taught in many elementary schools, and her last position was as the periodicals librarian at Thomas More College.

Joseph and Clara Ruschmann had 11 children—nine girls and two boys. Three of the girls entered St. Walburg Monastery. Sr. Joseph (right) served as a cook her whole life, cooking at Madonna Manor from 1964 to 1986. After she retired, she continued baking pies and bread until 1999, when she moved to the monastery infirmary. Sr. Agnes (left) served as a cook and housekeeper in various places from 1939 to 1958 before becoming a housemother for boarders at Villa Madonna Academy, an occupational therapist for senior sisters at the monastery, and the director of senior citizens at St. Benedict's Parish. From 1951 to 1983, Sr. David (center) was the director of nursing and anesthesia in many of the community's hospitals. From 1983 to 1995, she was a nurse anesthetist at Clark Regional Medical Center in Winchester, Kentucky. From 1995 to 2006, she worked with the outreach program at St. Elizabeth Catholic Church in Ravenna, Kentucky.

All of the Wolking sisters came to St. Walburg Monastery. They are, from left to right, (first row) Srs. Charles and Teresa Wolking; (second row) Srs. Amelia, Mary Anne, Consolata, and Mercedes Wolking. Sr. Mary Anne taught elementary school, junior high school, and high school math and science, as well as teaching at Villa Madonna Montessori. Sr. Teresa was discussed on page 109. Sr. Amelia spent all of her life in service on the property, working as a seamstress, a dorm mother, a maintainer of the pool in the 1907 building, a laundress, and a cafeteria supervisor at VMA. Sr. Mercedes taught kindergarten, elementary school, and junior high school, doing kitchen and housekeeping work at Madonna Manor and multiple jobs at the monastery. Sr. Consolata served in the community's hospitals from 1954 to 1961. She was a surgical nurse at St. Elizabeth Hospital from 1965 to 1974. She was licensed in enterostomal therapy and established an ET department at Providence Hospital in Cincinnati. After that, she freelanced, working out of Schwartz Drugs in Florence. Sr. Charles, the last Wolking sister to enter the community, is featured on page 89.

The three Gough sisters came from a large family. Sr. Denise (back) graduated from St. Elizabeth Hospital School of Nursing and later trained as a nurse anesthetist in St. Cloud, Minnesota. She served in many of the community hospitals and, from 1975 to 2005, served at St. Clare Regional Medical Center in Morehead, Kentucky. Sr. Margaret Mary (front, right) is featured on page 92. Sr. Stella Marie (front, left) taught in various elementary schools from 1958 to 1974, after which she was the principal and the religious education coordinator at Mary, Queen of Heaven School, the executive director at Villa Madonna Academy, and the religious education coordinator at St. Henry Parish. From 1988 to 2004, she was the associate director of catechetical services for the Diocese of Covington. She serves the community now as the monastery and infirmary coordinator.

Two generations of the Frisch family came to St. Walburg Monastery. Sr. Elizabeth (front) is featured on page 103. Her two nieces, Sr. Jeanette (back, left) and Anne (back, right) joined her in 1946 and 1949, respectively. Sr. Jeanette was a housemother at St. John Orphanage, an elementary schoolteacher, and an LPN in the community's healthcare facilities. In 1991, she received a BA in Gerontology. In her retirement years, Sr. Jeanette has been an active volunteer in many organizations. Sr. Anne served as an elementary schoolteacher and a librarian in many schools. From 1980 to 1995, she served as a teacher's aide at Villa Madonna Montessori.

Seven

Prayer and Community Life

People are often curious about how religious women pray and live. This chapter provides a peak into the everyday life of the sisters at St. Walburg Monastery over time. Prayer is the center of Benedictine life. The community's common prayer together is the public prayer of the Church: Eucharist and the Liturgy of the Hours.

In Eucharist, the community makes its own Christ's obedient offering of Himself to God and celebrates its communion with the Body of Christ.

In his Rule, Benedict calls Liturgy of the Hours the "Work of God" and directs that nothing be preferred to it. The SWM community gathers together at regular times for morning prayer, noonday prayer, evening prayer, and night prayer. The Liturgy of the Hours consists of psalms, hymns, Old and New Testament canticles, readings from Scripture, intercessions, and prayers. Through the celebration of Liturgy of the Hours, the community gives "voice to the prayer of the Church in praise and supplication."

In addition to public prayer, each member of the community gives herself time each day for *lectio divina*, or sacred reading, a Benedictine form of reading Scripture in a meditative and prayerful way.

Community life is a priority for Benedictine women. SWM is a community of women who pray together, eat together, laugh together, and seek God together. There are meetings with the whole community about once a month as well as community retreats and even parties. The sisters make decisions together that affect the whole community.

Above, the community prays the Liturgy of the Hours in the monastery chapel in the 1950s. When the sisters came to the United States, they prayed the Little Office of the Blessed Virgin Mary because it was shorter and left them with more time for their work of education. It was not until 1938 that SWM started to pray the entire Divine Office in Latin. Bishop Howard gave the community permission to recite the Divine Office "in so far as it will not interfere with teaching." Below is a page from the Office book for the celebration of First Vespers for the Feast of St. Benedict on March 21.

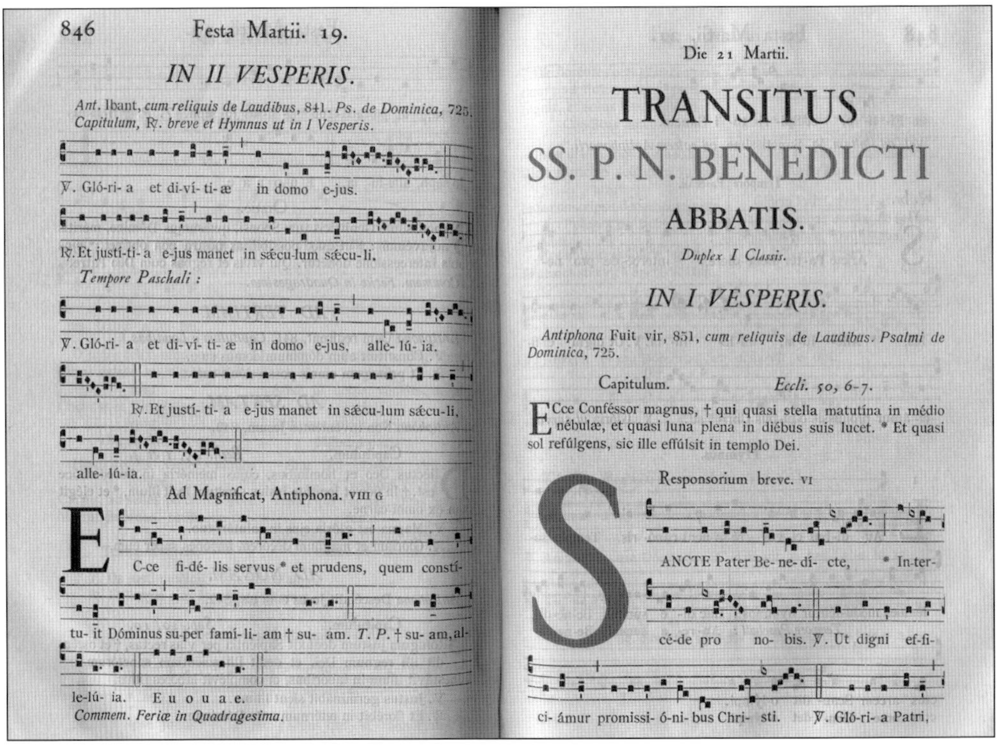

846 Festa Martii. 19.

IN II VESPERIS.

Ant. Ibant, *cum reliquis de Laudibus*, 841. *Ps. de Dominica*, 725. *Capitulum*, ℟. *breve et Hymnus ut in I Vesperis.*

℣. Gló-ri- a et di-ví- ti- æ in domo e-jus.

℟. Et justí-ti- a e-jus manet in sǽcu-lum sǽcu-li.

Tempore Paschali :

℣. Gló-ri- a et di-ví- ti- æ in domo e-jus, alle- lú- ia.

℟. Et justí- ti- a e-jus manet in sǽcu-lum sǽcu-li, alle- lú-ia.

Ad Magnificat, Antiphona. VIII G

E C-ce fi-dé- lis servus * et prudens, quem constí- tu- it Dóminus su-per fami-li- am † su- am. *T. P.* † su- am, al- le-lú- ia. E u o u a e.

Commem. Feriæ in Quadragesima.

Die 21 Martii.

TRANSITUS

SS. P. N. BENEDICTI

ABBATIS.

Duplex I Classis.

IN I VESPERIS.

Antiphona Fuit vir, 851, *cum reliquis de Laudibus. Psalmi de Dominica*, 725.

Capitulum. *Eccli.* 50, 6-7.

Ecce Confessor magnus, † qui quasi stella matutina in médio nébulæ, et quasi luna plena in diébus suis lucet. * Et quasi sol refúlgens, sic ille effúlsit in templo Dei.

Responsorium breve. VI

S ANCTE Pater Be- ne- dí- cte, * In-ter- cé-de pro no- bis. ℣. Ut digni ef-fi- ci- ámur promissi- ó-ni- bus Chri- sti. ℣. Gló-ri- a Patri,

Looking at the page from the Liturgy of the Hours book (previous page), it is obvious that it was necessary to obtain some instruction in singing and praying it. Singing practice has always been part of the preparation for Eucharist and Liturgy of the Hours. Here, Sr. Marcella Fedders teaches postulants and novices how to sing and pray in the 1950s.

Musicians are vital to the life of a Benedictine community. Sr. Colleen Winston (pictured) is the musician for most of SWM's public prayer. Sr. Colleen has two master's degrees: one in biology, and one in communications and theology. She taught from 1959 to 1974 before becoming a freelance media consultant, workshop presenter, and slide-program producer. From 1981 to 1988, she worked as the director of communications for the Diocese of Covington. Sr. Colleen coordinates liturgy preparation with other members of the community.

In 1964, the community began to pray the Divine Office in English. Because there was no common English translation of the Divine Office for Benedictines, the community used a book titled *Prayer for Christians* and other books prepared by community members. In 1989, after the renovation of the chapel, a committee was established to produce new Liturgy of the Hours books. The community began using the new books, seen below, in 1991.

Prayer is part of a Benedictine community's life in every season. Above, the community takes part in a Rogation Day procession in the 1950s. Rogation Days were days set aside to ask God's grace for a good and bountiful harvest. The major Rogation Day is April 25, and there are three minor days before the Feast of the Ascension. On special occasions, such as Palm Sunday, the community gathers in the front entrance of the monastery (below). Guests are always welcome, especially at Eucharist and Liturgy of the Hours.

Eating meals together is part of community life. These teaching sisters prepare to eat together at Holy Cross Parish in the 1940s.

Not all meals together are formal. This "powder milk biscuit" picnic was held in front of the guesthouse in the early 1980s.

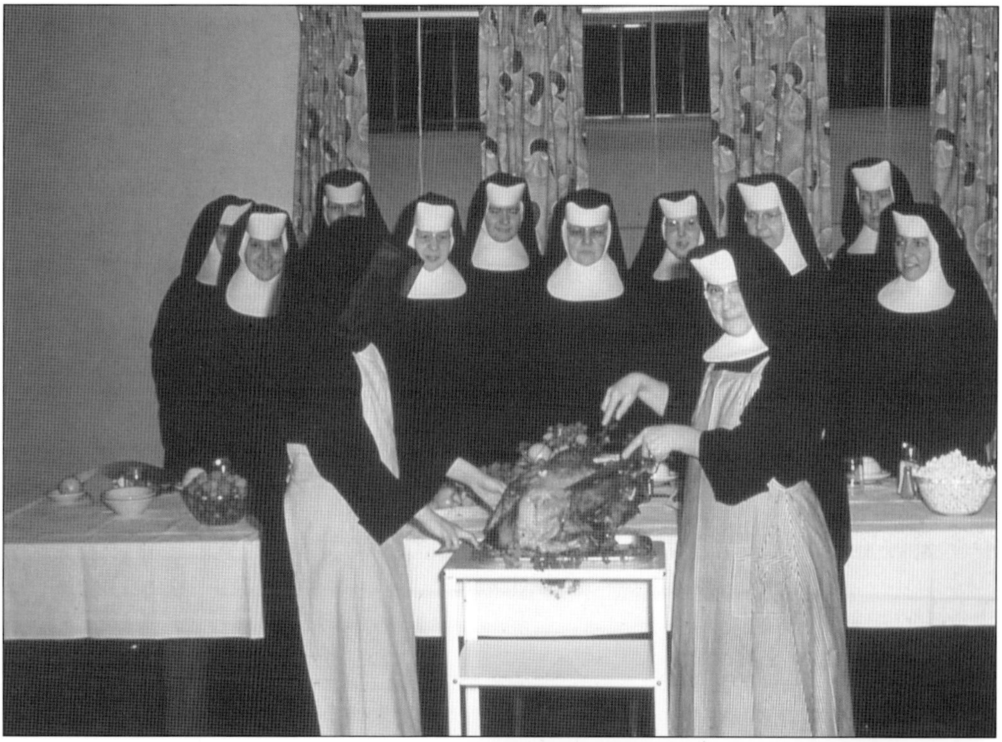

The cook is an important person in the life of a Benedictine community. Above, Sr. Anselma Weibel, the cook at Holy Cross, shows off her turkey at the 1956 Thanksgiving dinner.

Sr. Rita Bilz was the cook at St. Walburg Monastery from 1962 to 2006. Sr. Rita's usual Wednesday supper menu of fried chicken and homemade pie was always something to look forward to. Even though she is retired, Sr. Rita continues to make pies for Wednesday evening suppers.

Meals include lots of dishes. Seen here from front to back, Srs. Clarita Anneken, Barbara Woeste, Mary Carol Hellmann, and Martha Walther clean up in the monastery kitchen.

When community members get together, there is a lot of laughter. Here, from left to right, Srs. Agnes Ruschmann, Nancy Kordenbrock, Immaculata Campbell, Esther O'Hara, Pauline Rice, Mary Anne Wolking, and Martha Feder enjoy a good time together in the 1980s.

In Benedictine communities, the members discuss and make decisions together. Formal decisions are made in Chapter, the meeting in which the prioress calls the whole community together to listen, discuss, and make decisions. This small group, meeting in the monastery's lower level in the 1980s, includes, clockwise from bottom left, Srs. Amelia Wolking, Concetta Robinson, Henrietta Seiler, Nancy Kordenbrock, and Dorothy Schuette. The other three sisters cannot be identified.

Group trips are also a part of community life. These sisters took a weekend trip to Cumberland Falls from their home at Villa Madonna Academy in the 1970s.

Community celebrations call for festive cakes. Above, Sr. Joan Fraenzle, whose past ministries include working as a lab technician in hospitals and as an activities director in nursing homes, is one of the sisters who bakes and decorates cakes. Sr. Joan also helps with driving sisters who cannot drive to doctors' appointments and other places. She bakes once or twice a week in the monastery kitchen.

Sr. Christa Kreinbrink (left) has an MSA in nonprofit management from the University of Notre Dame and has been the monastery's director of buildings and grounds since 1982. She is the supervisor of the monastery's maintenance department and has been the owner's representative in the monastery's two renovations as well as the air-conditioning and window-replacement projects.

In 1987, a group of 28 women and men began the Benedictine Associate Program, with Sr. Martha Walther as program director. The Benedictine Sisters invited "Christian men and women of various lifestyles, who wish to bond together with the Benedictine Sisters and to 'truly seek God' according to the vision of St. Benedict." The program was later renamed the Benedictine Oblate program, "oblate" being a monastic term used to designate laypeople affiliated in prayer with a monastery of their choice. The Oblates have opportunities throughout the year for sharing, service, and celebration with the sisters. The yearly commitment is called an oblation and is celebrated annually. At the 2006 Oblation in the monastery chapel, Jerry Lockhart (far left) and Mike Page (second from left) approach the altar.